Praise for Untangled

Untangled is a powerful resource for anyone navigating change, whether it's the change we choose or the change we don't. Kirsty Maynor's practical tools, inspiring stories, and journalling prompts provide readers with the skills and insight they need to find meaning and purpose in any situation.

Jack Canfield, Legendary Self-Esteem Expert, Originator 'Chicken Soup for the Soul' series & New York Times Best-selling Author

---

In Untangled, Kirsty Maynor brings a business mindset to personal growth. Her compelling professional and personal experience of change has put her in the boardrooms of companies around the world. In this book, she brings that expertise directly to you. If you're facing change and don't know where to start, you've come to the right place.

Sean Gallagher, Entrepreneur, Dragons' Den Investor, Best-selling Author & Two Time Irish Presidential Candidate

Kirsty's a brave, quirky and brilliant leader. I've known her for 10 years and would trust her to lead you through change with integrity, compassion and wisdom. Untangled can be the guide by your side, steadying you in life's turbulence.

Henry Kimsey-House, Founder, Co-Active Training Institute (www.coactive.com)

I admire Kirsty and her work in the world as a force for good, including this lovely and inspiring book. Untangled has all the ingredients to become an invaluable toolkit for meeting the challenges of a conscious life.

Barnet Bain, Academy-Award Winning Film Producer, Emmy Award Nominee, Faculty Member, Columbia University and Author, 'The Book of Being and Doing'

As someone deeply committed to personal growth and empowerment, I fully endorse Untangled by Kirsty Maynor. This book is a powerful resource for anyone seeking to untangle the complexities of change, whether it's by choice or circumstance. It's filled with valuable tools and insights to help you thrive.

Vanessa Vallely OBE, Author,Inspirational Speaker & Entrepreneur, Co-Founder 'WeAreTheCity

In the vast realm of talent and expertise, Kirsty Maynor stands out as a beacon of brilliance. Her contributions to the world are not just transformative, they are also deeply rooted in a wealth of unparalleled experience. Among the myriad of self-help books that flood the market, Untangled emerges as a radiant diamond, infusing your life with sparkle. It's not just a book; it's an invitation. An invitation to grant yourself the freedom to navigate life's changes with profound clarity, genuine connection, and empowered choices. Don't merely read—immerse yourself. Begin the journey of untangling the complexities of your life today!

Patty Aubery, Past President of Chicken Soup for the Soul Enterprises, #1 New York Times Best-selling Author of 'Chicken Soup for the Working Woman's Soul' and President of The Jack Canfield Companies.'

Kirsty Maynor's Untangled shines with wisdom, an uplifting guide to navigating life's changes with joy.

Marci Shimoff, #1 New York Times Best-selling Author, Happy for No Reason and Chicken Soup for the Woman's Soul

---

Untangled by Kirsty Maynor isn't just a read—it's a strategic asset for conquering change, stacking the odds in your favor. Kirsty's corporate and personal experience shines throughout, she's a catalyst for entrepreneurs and anyone facing change.

Colin Sprake, CEO & Founder, Make Your Mark Training & Consultancy Ltd, Four-times Best-selling Author

Encouraging, empowering and informative all at once. I would gift this brilliant guide to all the loved ones in my life, because it reshapes our relationship with change and inspires self-honesty and courage in every chapter.

Ken Honda, Japan's International Best-selling Author of Happy Money

---

Many of us go through life on autopilot, rarely pausing to reflect on our true desires and aspirations. But have you ever taken a moment to deeply contemplate what you genuinely seek from life? It's a daunting question, one that requires courage and introspection. If you're ready to embark on this profound journey of self-discovery, then Kirsty Maynor's book is the ideal companion to guide you. Untangled is not just another book; it's a comprehensive guide that delves deep into the intricate web of life's challenges and intricacies.

Kirsty's writing is captivating and insightful, making the reading experience enjoyable and enlightening. What sets Untangled apart is its practical approach to life's challenges. It doesn't just offer philosophical ideas; it provides actionable steps and strategies to navigate the ever-changing landscape of life. Whether you're facing personal, professional, or spiritual transitions, this book serves as the ultimate blueprint, helping readers not only understand but also adapt and thrive amidst change. I wholeheartedly recommend it to anyone seeking clarity, direction, and a deeper understanding of themselves and the world around them.

Gabriel Nossovitch, Chairman of the Board, Worldworks México, Co-Founder, Worldworks Inc

Untangled brings structure and intention to handling change. Kirsty's got a unique way of putting you in the driving seat of change with practical tools, clarity and relatability. A valuable addition to any self-help library.

Dr. Ivan Misner, Founder of BNI and New York Times Best-selling Author

---

'In Untangled, Kirsty Maynor brings a business mindset to personal growth. Her compelling professional and personal experience of change has put her in the boardrooms of companies around the world. In this book, she brings that expertise directly to you. If you're facing change and don't know where to start, you've come to the right place.

Lisa Nichols, #1 New York Times Best-selling Author, Chicken Soup for the African American Soul, No Matter What!: 9 Steps to Living the Life You Love and Abundance Now: Amplify Your Life & Achieve Prosperity Today

Untangled

A practical and inspirational guide to change we choose and change we don't

Kirsty Maynor

Matador
Unit E2 Airfield Business Park,
Harrison Road, Market Harborough,
Leicestershire. LE16 7UL
Tel: 0116 2792299
Email: books@troubador.co.uk
Web: www.troubador.co.uk/matador
Twitter: @matadorbooks

ISBN 978 1805141 501

British Library Cataloguing in Publication Data.
A catalogue record for this book is available from the British Library.

Printed and bound by CPI Group (UK) Ltd, Croydon, CR0 4YY
Typeset in 11pt Adelle Condensed by Bhavini Lakhani.

Matador is an imprint of Troubador Publishing Ltd

MIX
Paper | Supporting
responsible forestry
FSC www.fsc.org
FSC® C171272

For three women whose tangles are forever woven together with mine

My mum, Carolyn,

My granny, May,

& my daughter, Scarlet

With endless love

K

A Tangled Mess

Atticus Poetry, *Love Her Wild*

She was the most beautiful
Complicated thing
I'd ever seen.
A tangled mess
Of silky string.
And all I wanted of life,
Was to sit down
Cross-legged
And untie her knots.

Disclaimer

This book is not a substitute for getting appropriate and qualified support if you are struggling with your mental health. If you feel that you would benefit from working with a trained professional, please see your doctor or a licensed therapist or psychologist. Asking for help is a sign of strength – it shows that you know when you can benefit from other people – and there are a lot of great professionals who are ready to help you as soon as you ask.

The stories shared in this book are drawn from over twenty-five years of working with individuals, teams and organisations. Examples of individuals facing change are never solely based on one individual client; they are a combination of stories to protect confidentiality and anonymity. Names have been made up and any identifying features are combined from a number of clients. My clients may recognise some of themselves in these stories, and I hope that this serves them to remember that they are never the only one experiencing a challenge – many others are in very similar positions. As one illustrative example, the story about a client struggling to identify their strengths is a story I could write about at least several people every single year.

I have also shared my own story. As with any of our human memories, these are likely to have evolved over time, and what is shared here is my current articulation of my story.

Contents

Part 1: Untangling the Myths

Part 2: Untangling Your Path

Part 3: Untangling Your Way

Chapter 5: How to Handle Your Feelings Through Change

Introduction

- What if the whisper in your heart was showing you what you truly want?
- What if you could actually make that change a reality?
- What if you could finally get out of your own way and overcome the barriers that have kept you where you are?

Welcome to *Untangled*!

I'm Kirsty Maynor and I'm here to help make any change you face right now, and in the future, easier to deal with. I'll help you to finally take the steps to create change you long for in your life, and I can also be your guide through the uncertainty of change that you would never have chosen, but have to deal with anyway.

Together in the pages that follow we'll gently tease apart the threads of your life, unravel the knots and choose the threads that you want to weave into your future. In doing so, you'll discover tools and skills that will help you in the months and years to come.

We'll gently tease apart the threads of your life, unravel the knots and choose the threads that you want to weave into your future

---

I believe you've picked up this book because the chances are you have things in your life that you wish were different, what I call *proactive* change. You're probably also dealing with change that life has thrown at you, also known as *reactive* change. It might surprise you to know that the contents of this book will help you with both.

The approaches, tools and skills I'm sharing with you here are the same I've used to help thousands of leaders in organisations to handle change, as well as what's helped me in my own personal and professional life. I've been through changes I've chosen, like building a dream home, setting up an award-winning business and relationship changes. I've also had my fair share of changes that I would never have chosen, like losing my job, the death of my mum and being a single parent for over eight years. What I've seen time and time again is that these things are not clean and tidy, they're messy and imperfect and they usually force us to face some of the things in ourselves that we'd rather not look at closely. I've also come to realise that, if we have support with change in our lives, we can come through it with more resources available to us for the future. And, even more powerfully, the skills and tools we need for change we choose, are in fact the same as those we need for change we don't.

My deepest hope is that, through reading this book, you remember that you are not alone. Whether you hold a secret desire to change careers, or you just want to start to move your body more, there are many others around the world feeling the same fears, facing the same barriers and trying to decide every day if they actually are going to do this thing. And if you're facing change that has been thrown at you, I absolutely guarantee you this: whatever you're feeling, and the challenges you face, they are the same ones as many others are facing right now. Human beings are very good at thinking they are alone and the only one. 'I thought it was just me' is such a common phrase I hear in coaching sessions. It's not. It never was. It never will be. You are not alone.

To make the most of the contents of this book is going to take work. You can read the book; the stories will inspire you; the tools and skills will spark some thinking. And nothing huge will change for you. If you're serious about giving yourself more insight and changing your forward path, it's going to take effort from you too. What I mean by that, is that it takes a little time and space to reflect more deeply on yourself, your life, the change you're facing and how it fits together so that you know different, and can choose different, from here on in.

So, before we even start, let's set you up for success:

Decide when you'll make space for you and the knotted, tangled change you're facing – it can be ten minutes a day or bigger chunks of time. Choose now and write it into your planner or calendar (and if that needs to change and evolve, that's okay – start with what you think will work for now).

Gather together what you'll need to work through this book. You'll want a pen or two and a separate notebook to write your thoughts in. There's a beautiful *Untangled* journal with all the journal prompts if you'd like to have them easily to hand. You can order it at all good book shops or through the *Untangled* website (*www.untangledbook.com*), and there are also free downloadable resources available, including a checklist for the whole book and examples in case you get stuck.

Commit to staying curious and being as kind to yourself as you can be. Facing change isn't easy – you might need to learn more about how to be your own source of support, and you're probably going to need to learn to ask for help a bit more than you might have in the past. You'll experience a range of emotions as you work through this book and live through change. Be gentle with yourself – you matter.

Choose how you will respond. What's included in these pages works, and it needs be on your terms. Any question or journal prompt, any activity, any challenge that I've set out, is all up to you to take and use in a way that serves you best. You always have the right to choose, to go with it, to say 'no' or to find a different way. Make this work for you. This is your life and your change.

Tell someone what you're doing. The more accountability you have for change you face, the more likely it is to happen. And you'll have support, so it doesn't always feel so tough. So, pick up your phone and let someone know you are reading this book because you want to equip yourself for change. I'm sure that person will want to help you; you just need to let them.

One small note if you're facing change you haven't chosen and it's life-altering, like a close bereavement, the loss of your job or a major health issue. You might find Parts 2 and 3 feel out of reach for you just now, and that's okay. Start by using the sections in Part 4 and possibly the content in Chapter 6 on letting go, to support you in handling your feelings and any current barriers. Come back to Parts 2 and 3 when you're feeling a little more ready to start to peek around the corner at your potential future. I'll help you start to slowly explore what might be here for you in your new reality.

My Promise

My promise to you is simple: the contents of this book will give you the inspiration, tools, skills and resources to live through any kind of change you choose and change you don't with courage, connection, choices and clarity.

This book will change your life, but only if you want it to.

Kirsty

Notes

About Journalling

Throughout this book you'll find journalling prompts to help you think more deeply and reflect on the content. The act of reflection helps you to have more insight, and from that enhanced understanding, you can take different action in the future. When we write things down, we get them out of our head and on to paper. Our thoughts, feelings and beliefs pass from our heads to our hearts through our hands.

As Stephen M.R. Covey says in *Trust and Inspire* '...just because we are immersed in something, it doesn't need to be how we operate. Once we see clearly...we can choose to operate differently.' This is the power of journalling, it helps us to see clearly our own thoughts and feelings. Once we can see them, we have more choice.

Journalling might be new to you, or you might be someone who's been writing for years. Either way, in the context of *Untangled*, I wanted to offer a few thoughts and tips to help release you from anything that might get in the way of you picking up a pen or pencil and starting to write your thoughts.

You can't get it wrong

Journalling isn't about the right spelling or grammar. It's not about writing in order to create some Pulitzer-winning body of work. The act of taking some time to yourself, picking up a pen and seeing what flows off the end of it, is an act of connection to yourself, for yourself. There is no right way to journal. You might simply make marks on the paper. There might not even be any words. You might write random words in spaces on the page. You might connect them. Or not. Perhaps you'll write a sentence. Maybe pages will flow without you realising. One day you may find yourself writing the same things over and over again. Let it all happen. It's all moving you closer to clarity about yourself and this life you're living.

It's helpful to have a space to write

And I mean this in two ways. Firstly, it can be helpful to have a journal or notebook that you can use to gather your thinking into one place. I've scribbled journalling-type content on sticky notes, scraps of paper, and it never feels quite right to me. I worry that the words and thoughts will get lost. So, give yourself a tangible, physical way to keep things together. It also makes it easier to spot patterns and themes and to look back and see your evolution. I designed the Untangled Journal specifically for this purpose. The second type of space is space in your life and in your day or week. It doesn't need to be much; even setting a timer for ten minutes can start to transform the insight and perspective you get from connecting with yourself. Choose a time that you can commit to and start from there. If all you can do is write down three sentences at the end of the day in a book that you keep by your bed, start there. If you realise that writing a word for how you're feeling each morning when you make your first cup of tea or coffee brings you new insight, start there. Just start.

Make it your own

Both of the above centre on one thing. Make journalling work for you. Do it your way. You'll find tons of ideas, prescriptions and instructions online. And they can be helpful starting points if you're completely new to writing down the contents of your head and heart. But don't let them constrain you. Find your own way. This is your space and time for you. You get to choose how to create a practice that brings you pleasure and peace.

I'm totally delighted that we have a companion journal available for *Untangled*. I created it so that if you'd like to have the journalling prompts together in one space that you can work through, you can do so. It's an inspirational resource for you to pick up each day if it helps you. And I also love stationery, so if you want to go out and find yourself a beautiful notebook to use, feel free. Again, pick something that feels positive for you and keeps you coming back to pick up your pen each day.

Notes

PART 1

UNTANGLING THE MYTHS

Notes

Chapter 1:
Untangling the Myths of Change

Introduction

I've often struggled with huge self-doubt. Some people would call this imposter syndrome, the doubting of my own skills and accomplishments. Many mornings I've woken up with the icky feeling that I was going to get caught out, that everyone would realise I wasn't as good as they had thought I was, or even good at all. I used to think the tiniest mistake would mean my employer would fire me. So, it wasn't a surprise to my then husband when I called him one day at lunchtime and said, 'I think they're going to fire me'. With casual disregard, he replied, 'Well, you've thought that before and they never have. What's happened this time?'

This time felt different. I hadn't actually done anything wrong, but my boss had summoned me to a meeting that afternoon. Since I was due to meet with a client, I went to ask my boss's assistant, a friend of mine, if the meeting could be moved. She opened his diary to see if it could be changed, and I noticed that my HR representative's details were also in the calendar – she was flying up from London to Edinburgh in only a few hours' time. A sinking feeling told me this was not good news. We barely saw her; in fact, I don't remember any other visits before that day. My stomach lurched. Could this be the end of the road? Still, my husband reassured me that I was overreacting and reminded me that I had done nothing wrong. Giving myself a shake, I told myself it was probably unrelated and carried on through my meetings.

Come 4pm, I was still feeling edgy so I entered that meeting room with a little trepidation, legs slightly less stable than I would have liked them to be. Sitting opposite me were my boss and the HR representative. *Ah. This is the end of the road.* I don't remember the details of what was said; I do remember the feeling of the life draining out of my body and feeling completely numb with shock. This was 2008, the start of the global recession, and I was the first of many casualties, but it didn't make it any easier to handle. I hadn't done anything wrong, but I had lost my job. And as the sole earner in our household, with a three-year-old daughter, this was not good news. Two weeks before Christmas, I felt I didn't even know who I was any more, where to turn or how to pick myself up.

'Put the champagne in the fridge – I've just been fired'

Leaving the office, I tried to stop the tears, gather myself together. I called my husband and did the only thing I felt I could. 'Put the champagne in the fridge – I've just been fired,' I said, my voice cracking. I realise that might sound odd, so let me explain a little. Firstly, I always try to always have a bottle of some wine with bubbles – Prosecco or sometimes champagne – available in case a celebration arises. Secondly, the only thing I could do at that point, was to trust that this was the start of something better. I was completely out of control; my job, and to a large extent, my existence, had been pulled from under my feet. I had no idea what was next. I felt betrayed, mistreated and badly hurt. But what I could control was my reaction to it, at least on that day. There were many days of anger, tears, sadness, hurt and much more in the weeks to come. And on that day, the only thing that I felt I could do was to raise a glass to my future. Because it started on that day, and I was about to learn that most of what I'd been taught about how to handle change, just didn't work for me.

You see, I was a specialist in change – I think my shiny business cards from the big-four consulting firm I worked for even said 'Change Management Consultant'. Organisations paid big money to get me to work with them and tell them how to manage change they wanted to make. I had PowerPoint presentations with fancy diagrams. I had read the books and academic literature. I had listened to famous people like Tom Peters, Peter Drucker and Rosabeth Moss-Kanter talking about the things that mattered in change. I had even studied it at university. But, as I was about to discover, none of it helped me. Me, the main, okay the only, earner in the household. Me, a parent to a three-year old who kept us busy. Me, who had only just recently recovered from postpartum depression. Me, who lacked self-belief and had no idea what I was really capable of. The standard things I knew about change didn't help me. They were all lies, or myths. Things that sounded good on paper but didn't work in practice. Advice created largely by middle-aged men with wives at home to take care of everything. Tips generated from a world that might as well have been an alien planet. So here, let me share those myths with you, why they don't work for me and what the reality actually looks like.

I'm starting with these because they matter. Whether you're facing change that life has thrown at you, or you're choosing to make some shifts in your world, we need to clear the ground. These myths get in the way. Before we can start to untangle your path and your way forward, we need to make sure that these are not going to stop you in your tracks. From personal experience, I know that when we get caught up in these myths, it can hold us back. Each of these pieces of received wisdom is enough to stop us from moving forward. So, let's bust the myths and then we can get going. I'll share the myths and how I see the reality to let you start clearing the ground for yourself. I've included some journal prompts at the end of the section which you can use if it's helpful to get clarity for yourself before you move on.

Myth 1: You have to take a giant leap

Most people think you have to cross in one giant leap. There will be no baby steps here. I mean, even when the steps are small, they get exaggerated. I'm looking at you, Neil Armstrong. I'm not actually against taking giant leaps where they really, truly are the only way. But most of the time, the idea of having to take a mega jump is enough to make us freeze. Not because we are scared – though sometimes that's true – but more because we often have so much to lose. The act of taking both feet off the ground and leaving the planet momentarily (because that's what leaping actually entails) just doesn't seem feasible. And it isn't

> Sometimes your biggest achievement is just to keep breathing, and that's okay

necessary most of the time. We can face change by building out scaffolding, by making it possible to take smaller steps. Heck, sometimes we can even live through change by getting down on our hands and knees and crawling, keeping going, no matter what. In fact, sometimes that is the only way, particularly for the kind of change that life throws at us. So, let's not pretend that we need to be taking giant leaps and changing the world overnight. Even with the biggest changes we choose, like leaving relationships or changing career, we can create a path to move us on. Let's crawl if we have to, but keep moving. And if you're facing change that you would never have chosen, this applies tenfold. Sometimes your biggest achievement is just to keep breathing, and that's okay.

Myth 2: You need self-belief

Self-belief is required to live through change. Actually, the truth is it's often waiting on the other side of the change. We're told we have to believe in ourselves, and the assumption is that if we don't, we should hold off on starting our own business, relocating or making some other moves in our lives. Yet so often, in reality, it's only when we look back at the changes we have made, that we can say, 'I never would have thought it was possible; I didn't believe I could achieve it'. The self-belief comes from the change. The change does not come from the self-belief. I've seen this time and time again in my own life. So often, I doubt myself every step of the way until I get to the other side, and then I wonder how I managed it. It's even happening with this book. I keep taking the steps, even on the days when I don't believe I can do it. Word by word, page by page, I keep going. And then, when I've written more, edited more, I realise that I can do it. In fact, I am doing it. And so can you. This links closely to myth 3...

Myth 3: You have to have complete clarity

The next myth of change is that you need to have complete clarity about what you want, before you start out to create change in your lives. Now that might work if you live in a world where you have tons of time to yourself. But if you're anything like most busy people I know, if you wait until you have the time to figure out the details, you'll be halfway through your life before you even get started on making it a reality. Even if you could carve out time to do that, how you imagine the reality is often so different to what emerges. You'd have wasted your time. Better to start somewhere, take some baby steps and then see what happens as you work out where to go from there. Sometimes this myth applies to the end result of the change we want to create; sometimes it relates to the way we're going to make that happen.

My daughter Scarlet and I had that experience in tangible form when we went on a trip to New York. I always think it shouldn't be easy for me to get lost in a grid system, but somehow I manage it. After we'd walked for a few blocks south, quite a few, we were both starting to get tired and grouchy. We knew where we were heading; a friend had recommended we go to Chelsea Market and walk the elevated skyline to get good views of the city. I'd decided we'd walk through the city on the way down, and then back on the skyline. It is not a good idea! We ended up walking through some parts of Manhattan that were, let's just say, less than picturesque. The grumpiness grew, my nagging voice telling me I'd made the wrong decision and was ruining part of our holiday. Scarlet and I started a discussion about how to navigate when you're lost. It turns out we have completely different strategies. She is much more inclined to stop, plan out a route and know exactly which way she's going. She likes the clarity. On the other hand, I'm much more likely to set an intention, an idea of where I'm going, and then take steps to go there, adjusting as I need to, heading in the right overall direction but open to what shows up on the way. Neither one is more right than the other – they are different journeys, but often lead to the same destination. I just want to remind you, that you don't have to have it all figured out before you get started. We made it to Chelsea Market. It was worth it – we had a very tasty lunch and did some shopping. We even found a cool book and stationery shop which is (as you may already know) pretty much my idea of heaven. And we're still talking, so the grumpiness didn't linger. In fact as I finish the work on this book she is getting ready for university. You don't need to have complete clarity. If you feel like you've got it, that's great. If not, don't let it stop you. Tune in to the feeling you have, the dream you may hold or the compelling feeling that you have to move forward. And start with that.

You don't
need to have
complete clarity

Myth 4: You need to get less sleep

You have to get less sleep. The way to prioritise yourself through change is to get less sleep. Yup. Really. I'm talking about the advice to get up even earlier, meditate, write and have moments of enlightenment before you even get the toast on the table. Believe me, I have tried early morning 'power hours' – they were not a strategic tool for success; they were an act of total desperation and resulted in me drinking more coffee, closing my eyes in the afternoon and a reluctance to read my daughter a(nother) bedtime story. The reality is, most people who balance multiple responsibilities would do better to carve out fifteen minutes somewhere in the day – even if it means you have to stick the kids in front of the TV for a cartoon or get a ready-made dinner. If you are serious about change, then you do need to make time for it and for yourself, but it doesn't have to be hours of stillness and contemplation. It needs to be when you are naturally awake and alert. Do the things that matter most when you are at your best. And you can still get sleep when you're going through change; in fact, I insist on it.

Myth 5: You have to be single-minded

You have to be single-minded. Well, maybe this works if you only have one priority. But that doesn't reflect the reality of life for most people I know and have worked with. We simply don't have the luxury of being able to shut out everything else and focus on the creation of the new habit or the job change. Even when we are adapting to change that life has thrown at us, we usually face the day-to-day things that most people need to do to survive like getting up, eating, food shopping, and putting the rubbish out. Unless you put your kids/pets/partner/parents in a box, we are multi-faceted, multi-potential, multi-responsible individuals. So, our way of living through change has to be multi-minded, with an understanding of how the parts fit together and what the priorities are in any given moment. I do find it helps to be single-minded at any one time. That means to be focused on one thing. As my daughter would tell you, if she's trying to talk to me and I'm in the middle of writing an email or planning my day, I can't focus on her. I know that when we have other commitments like children, pets or ageing parents it's extremely hard. To allow ourselves to be focused on something in any particular moment, we might need to ask someone to help or to accept that we just can't give our attention to the project we want to right now. And being multi-minded with multiple responsibilities might mean that we need to look at slightly bigger chunks of time.

> Set your goals in concrete but your timelines in sand

Ask yourself what you need over the course of this year. What matters to you this month? Look at how to weave these things together. Set your goals in concrete but your timelines in sand, and allow yourself to evolve.

Myth 6: It's either you or them

It's either you or them. And by them, I mean your partner, children, parents or others you care for, co-workers and others you connect with. I mean, it's tempting, but you're probably not about to ditch your family or friends in pursuit of your new future – unless that *is* your new future of course. You'll probably find the change a lot more meaningful and sustainable if you can include them in your plans and ideas from the outset. I've always involved my daughter in my business to some extent. As a single mum, I would have found it impossible to do anything else. She's known some of my team members and been to work dinners with them. It's given her skills such as being able to talk with adults from a very young age and to handle social situations that she might not otherwise have experienced. I remember one evening she came to dinner with a group of eight. We were meeting in person for the first time, ready to work with a client the next day. The team was my work coaching colleagues from the UK, USA and Dubai, and one of them even brought Scarlet a gift of stationery and chocolate. While I could have asked my parents to look after my daughter, who was nine at the time, I wanted to involve her in my project and for her to be connected with my life. I didn't always make the right decisions on that front, but integrating the different parts of my life has worked well and given us both much bigger gifts along the way.

Myth 7: You can drop all the other balls

You can drop the other balls while you focus on change – well, not if you're helping Granny and she needs her medication organised, or the kids are left at school because nobody picked them up! Know the balls you can drop or delegate, and know the ones you can't. Be prepared for this to evolve as you live through change. Sometimes it can be helpful to list all your roles and responsibilities. Your roles might include your job, your parenting or caring responsibilities; maybe you're a pet owner or a member of the local hockey team. Each of those will have responsibilities – write them down. Then mark which responsibilities are rubber balls, meaning they'll bounce if they get dropped. And then mark the ones that are crystal and will shatter if they hit the ground. You may be surprised to see that there are really very few that are absolutely vital to be done today. I need to do the grocery shopping today. I also need to edit this chapter. So, if I think about which of my responsibilities are essential, I realise I need to buy cat food and dog food because we will run out tonight. I could hold off buying the rest of my groceries or I could find a different way to get them. What's truly essential and what can you do differently, so that you can focus on the changes you want to create in your life? I'm going to leave the rest of the groceries today and concentrate on this chapter, because this book matters to me.

> Know the balls you can drop or delegate, and know the ones you can't

Myth 8: Change has to look good

Change has to look good – in the beginning, the middle and the end. In fact, it doesn't, and it won't. You don't need to look polished, put together or even to know what you're doing most of the time! Change is messy, and that's okay. Too often, we only see the end results of changes that others create in their lives. We don't see the doubt, the mountains they climbed or the struggles they've had to face. Posts on social media show the glossy version of the finish line. We see people holding up the book they've published. Friends share the successes of their children at school or in sports. Colleagues celebrate promotions and new jobs. What we don't see is that what happens between the starting point and the finish line often completely sucks. Like caterpillars turning into butterflies, the middle stage is often a gooey, sticky, deeply unpleasant mess. We doubt ourselves. There are tears and shouting. There's confusion and questioning if we're doing the right thing. Every single day we have to recommit. To get up, dust ourselves down and keep going. The big things we want in life don't come quickly and easily. Yes, there are things that can help to smooth the path. But if you're expecting this to look like three neat steps that you can follow without stepping in any puddles, taking any wrong turns or just wondering what you're even doing in the first place, I'm going to disappoint you. Change is not linear. Our lives are colourful, and that includes the icky bits. You will get there, and you are on the right track. Keep going. Especially when it's messy.

Myth 9: You have to drive change

You have to drive change. The reality is that, most of the time, change drives us from the inside and from the outside. All you can do is fasten your seatbelt. Attempts to believe we are running the show are futile. We can hang on, offer the occasional direction and trust that we'll get there. But in reality, change is the one in charge. Some of the biggest changes in my life have come when I've felt totally compelled to act, from the inside out. It didn't even feel like a conscious choice; I just knew I had to pursue a dream or an idea or a thought or, in the case of reactive change, I've just had to find a way forward. I often compare it to the stage when children become toddlers. Suddenly, this little person who I created starts to act completely independently. They stick toast into drawers, freeze their bodies solid when they don't want to do things, and generally run the show for a while. We have to work with them, respond to them, cling on and trust we'll get to the next stage. So, when you're facing change in your life, don't expect to feel in control all the time. As a reformed control freak, I understand that this can feel terrifying – try to just breathe. It's temporary. Let the change flow, and the less you resist it, the more will become possible.

Myth 10: You have to be kind to yourself

You have to be kind to yourself. Well, this last one is a bit of a trick. Ultimately, you do need to be kind to yourself. But that doesn't always look the way you think it might. The reality of self-care through change might mean making an appointment with your doctor, finding yourself a good therapist or actually nudging yourself to do the thing you don't want to do. It's not all about buying yourself the lilies or a new gadget. It can be those things, when they truly nourish you but, more often, it's about trying to treat yourself the way you'd treat others on a good day. In a sense, make yourself your own best friend. Sometimes that means you need tough love and boundaries. And sometimes, it means making a cup of coffee, sitting down and being honest with yourself about what you need.

When I was fired, I thought my world had ended. I also thought I knew how to cope with that seismic change. I was wrong on both counts. Since then, I've learned the real way to handle change, both the kind that I've chosen and the kind that has hunted me down when I least expected it. You can live through both kinds of change. You can even thrive through it. Put the champagne in the fridge (or

Make yourself your own best friend

a non-alcoholic equivalent), because we're raising a glass to your future. It starts today.

Summary

We have to clear the myths out of the way in order to give ourselves the best starting point. Even if we still believe in some of them to some extent, we need to put them to one side, clear the ground and step forward with the new reality.

Myth: You have to take a giant leap.

Reality: You can take baby steps or crawl if you have to.

Myth: You need self-belief.

Reality: Self-belief is waiting on the other side of the change.

Myth: You have to have complete clarity.

Reality: You can start with what you already know.

Myth: You need to get less sleep.

Reality: Sleep is vital.

Myth: You have to be single-minded.

Reality: You can be multi-minded and still find focus.

Myth: It's either you or them.

Reality: It's you *with* them.

Myth: You can drop all the other balls.

Reality: You can drop the rubber balls; they'll bounce.

Myth: Change has to look good.

Reality: Change doesn't look good in the messy middle.

Myth: You have to drive change.

Reality: Change will drive you; cling on.

Myth: You have to be kind to yourself.

Reality: You do have to be kind to yourself – it just might look different from what you've been told.

Journalling prompts

Which of the myths is hardest for you to release? What would be possible if you could put that myth to one side?

Reality 1: What's the first baby step you could take?

Reality 2: What would you dream of if you totally backed yourself?

Reality 3: What do you already know about what you want to create?

Reality 4: When is a good time of day for you to prioritise your future?

Reality 5: What else are you responsible for?

Reality 6: Who's in your world?

Reality 7: What are the balls you're juggling? Which ones would bounce?

Reality 8: In what ways do you still believe change has to look good?

Reality 9: What direction is the change taking you in?

Reality 10: What are the ways in which you're not kind to yourself yet?

Notes

Notes

Perspective,
Morgan Harper Nichols, *All Along You Were Blooming*

People change,

Seasons change,

And your perspective

Changes too...

You start to see

Where the light

Gets in.

And how

To make it

Through.

Notes

PART 2

UNTANGLING YOUR PATH

Notes

Chapter 2:
Clarify

Introduction

Now that we've cleared out those myths, it's time to settle into the three steps that help you to untangle your path: clarify, connect and choose. Remember, these are not clean, tidy, predictable steps. They're messy – some might be covered with moss and hard to find, and some might feel sticky and like you'll never move on from them. It's all okay. Even when it feels like it's not. It's part of being human and stumbling forward into the future; we create each day, with the choices we make.

While I believe the divine and destiny play their part, this is also a dance of two – you make the moves, and the universe responds

This is your life, and you are here to live it. I know that might sound obvious, but I wanted to remind you of this guiding truth now, right at the start. Because it can be easy to take for granted, or to forget, that each moment, each day, each week and each year is yours to design and live in accordance with your greatest purpose. You get to make the choices, the steps you'll follow, the paths you won't. And while I believe the divine and destiny play their part, this is also a dance of two – you make the moves, and the universe responds. It is not a foregone conclusion.

So take a deep breath now and listen. Pay attention to what you hear and also to what you don't. Notice what's in the space around you and within you. Breathe into your inner wisdom and remember that this is always available to you. As I guide you through these pages, on a path of discovering who you are, what you're here for and what truly matters to you, remember that your wisdom comes from within. These words are only here to act as an access point, a doorway to what's already inside you. And I start with you, because without you there is no here and now, and no there and then. The change that prompted you to pick up this book – chosen or otherwise – does not exist without you. So, I start with what's at the very centre. The beautiful human being who sits here now, perhaps uncertain, possibly lacking in confidence or self-belief, yet here, ready enough to move forward and live life more fully. Ready to face change.

This first section invites you to explore key aspects of yourself. Much of it might be new territory for you; you might have to pause and reflect, to get to know yourself differently. We start by looking at who you are, your purpose, your mission, your strengths, and what energises you so that you live through change in a way that has you at the centre. It helps to make sure that the change you choose is lasting, and it helps to give you guiding lights if you're facing change you didn't want to face. Each of these subsections can be read in a day. The work that goes with them, to reflect and take action, doesn't have to be done within a day. Take time if you need to, particularly if these questions are new to you. And make sure you actually do take the time, rather than put it off. You picked up this book because part of you is ready to become more intentional about how you live through change. That means you need to reflect and then put things into motion as a result. I believe you have it in you to do this work, even when it's hard going. I'm here to help you through it.

Who are you?

Let's start with who you are. This might seem a strange question if you picked up this book because you want to plan a house move or you're in the middle of reacting to losing your job. But let's imagine there's a 'yes... and...' possibility here. By which I mean you can, of course, move house and, in doing so, discover more about yourself and what matters to you in your life. The chances are, it'll make the house move more fulfilling and you might even stay there longer – if you want to. And if you're looking to make significant changes in your relationships or responding to the loss of a loved one, the question 'who are you?' might make more intuitive sense, even if you have no idea what the answers are. Because when we go through big changes, the kind that make it feel like the world has shifted on its axis, we often raise these questions, reaching to the very core of who we are and what our life is about. When my mum died suddenly in May 2021, I remember feeling like I had suddenly lost part of who I was. It felt like my heart had been ripped out and everything I had taken for granted and thought I knew no longer made sense, if it was even still there. I stopped eating, stopped sleeping. At times I felt like I forgot to breathe. My identity was gone. The person who'd been there since before I was born, wasn't there. We'd been estranged for a year in my twenties after long-term issues between us came to a dramatic head, but we'd worked hard to resolve that and, with the help of family therapy, by my thirties and forties we were closer than we'd ever been. Her death felt like the creation of a different paradigm. If she wasn't there anymore, who was I? It's no wonder I got lost driving around the city after she died. I was lost in my own self. I had to try to rediscover who I was in this new version of me. It took time. The reality is that I'm still in the discovery, and maybe I always will be. So be gentle with yourself if you are going through huge change. It doesn't happen overnight.

For today, I want to invite you to look at who you are – what do you know to be true about yourself? What matters to you most? Consider this a warm-up before we look at specific aspects of you in the coming chapters. We are starting with the general outline of you. Set a timer for each of these sentence stems and take three minutes to write down whatever comes up for you in response to the following prompts:

- I am a person who...
- At my core I...
- I want you to know that...

Since this is the first real journalling we're doing, and there will be more, the important thing to remember is that there is no wrong answer; just write down whatever comes into your mind. And if nothing comes to mind, then try to keep your pen on the page moving, even if you're writing the words 'I don't know what to write. What do I want to say?'. It doesn't matter if it doesn't make sense or if you don't write in full sentences. Nobody needs to be able to read the scribbles on the page, as long as you know what it says. The key is to start to tune in to what your subconscious mind has to say. Your conscious mind tends to run the show, but in navigating change we are looking to let all of you get involved. It might take a while, and that's okay; give yourself permission to take time and let the words flow. You might want to take yourself away, switch off your phone, or go for a walk, and see what comes to mind. It gets to be messy and imperfect, and whatever you come up with is valid. Give yourself permission to be bold and honest about what you want. And, if you'd like to keep all your thinking in one place, you can either get a separate notebook or a copy of the *Untangled* journal which has all of these prompts together in one beautiful place to hold your thoughts.

What's your purpose?

This section can be challenging for people. It might be too much for you just now, particularly if you're in the thick of life-altering change that has you struggling to even know which day it is. That's okay. Mark the page and come back to it. There's no rush. I'm including it here for those of you who want to dig deep and start with yourself, and we will also come back to this in Chapter 9 in more depth.

I never even thought about what my life purpose was until I first worked with my insightful coach Rama. Then I dipped my toe into the wonderful world of tools and ways of seeing life that have been created through co-active coaching. I was in my early thirties, and I had pretty much made a series of decisions throughout my life, one after another. I hadn't ever stopped to put the pieces together or to look at the threads that joined them. And there was absolutely nothing wrong with that. My life was fine; it wasn't broken. I was working with Rama because I wanted to get better at running a business that I'd started as a hobby. It was the first time I ever remember being in a conversation with someone where the only agenda was me. It felt so liberating to know that I wouldn't be judged. I felt free. I couldn't even see her – we were speaking on the phone. I felt safe to talk about what I wanted. I could share how I felt and explore my thoughts. I'd had a few coaching sessions with Rama, and I don't even remember what prompted us starting the work to look at my life purpose, but I do remember that, as we started to dig into why I'm here and what my bigger purpose is, something inside me sparked. What I had done up until then that had made me happy or brought me joy seemed to just fit. Things made more sense. I felt more aligned with my own self. More than a decade later, my life purpose continues to evolve and swirl, as I connect more deeply with who I am, and my role in this lifetime. And the foundations that appeared on that day gave me the starting point. So, let's find yours!

I'd like you to start by scanning your life so far, not the details, or the really painful bits, just a little glance back over the years to here. Think about which parts have made you feel most alive. If your life was to stop now, what difference would you have made? What would your story be? Let's write that story now, a short version. We're going to use a story spine, where all you do is write the ends of the sentences and use them to tell the story of your life to here. Simply fill out the ends of each of these sentences as if you were telling me the story of you:

- Once upon a time...
- Every day...
- Until one day...
- Because of that...
- Because of that...
- Because of that...
- (You can use this phrase as many times as you need to!)

And the moral of the story is...

- What do you notice about your life so far?
- What's the moral been?
- Why have you been here until now?

You may find this a bit difficult, so please be gentle with

You have a purpose, and you have meaning

yourself. This is absolutely not an opportunity for you to get a big stick out and beat yourself with it. It is not the time to start criticising what you've done with your life so far. Because you have a purpose, and you have meaning, and, even if you find it impossible to see, you have an impact, and you matter. I totally understand if it doesn't always feel like that. When we face life-altering change like health diagnoses or bereavement, or when we're facing challenges with our mental health, we can feel like we no longer have a purpose or have meaning. But I'm here to tell you that you do matter; you do have meaning; and there are many others who know you and love you who agree with me. So, if this feels too much and it's causing you anguish, please skip this section, come back to it another day and, if the pain and sense of meaninglessness continue, please consider seeking professional support from a trained counsellor, therapist or psychologist. You are worth taking that step. Your future self will thank you for it.

What do you stand for?

Now that we've taken an initial look at the broad landscape of you and your life, I want to invite you to take an early peek at what you stand for in the context of this change. Again, this might feel a strange thing to do at this stage, but a bit like when you paint a room, you're starting to put the colour on the walls, without getting into all the corners and crevices.

We're going to get clear on the thing you stand for, the thing you're willing to lay down your life for, whilst desperately hoping you don't have to. Think of it as your mission. In the context of navigating change, it becomes an expression of your purpose. When you're asked what you would do if you only had a short time to live, you think you know. But the reality is, if it happens, when it happens, your answer changes. And it is crystal clear. It's only the people who matter. So, when my mum was in the last few weeks of her life, my mission was to give her the best ending possible. We couldn't change the circumstances, but we could set an intention to guide us in our decisions and to rally other people around. For me, it was about giving Mum the best ending possible. In big ways and small. I was in a state of shock and disbelief. We all were. But it was time to act. To bring her as much joy as possible in the time she had. That mission meant I ordered brightly coloured umbrellas so that when we had to sit outside for visiting, due to the Covid-19 infection risk, we could do so without getting soaking wet. It also brightened up what was the most difficult of times in a tiny, but not unnoticeable, way. The same thing also guided us in the choice to show up and have difficult, but loving, conversations. It influenced the people my mum spent time with in her last few days in the hospice. Your mission might be for a smaller change, but it's still important to be clear on what you want from this stage in your life. If you're facing career change, what matters to you about how you handle that? Is it that you act with integrity and honour your value of honesty? Or is it that you give yourself as many options as possible and live the adventure of life? Or something else? The magical thing about a stake or mission is that it can't possibly be wrong – it's simply the guiding point for how you yourself take each step, so it can only ever be right.

> The magical thing about a stake or mission is that it can't possibly be wrong

- What's your mission for this change?

- What do you stand for?

- What would you write on a massive banner if you were
  on horseback and wanting people to follow you up
  the hill?

Write it down now and mark this page, because you will want to come back to it at points when you waver or when things get difficult. It will guide you, like the North Star. I've intentionally not included examples in the activities in this book because I want you to listen to your own inner knowing. If you're someone who finds it helpful to have examples, you can download a document with these at *www.untangledbook.com*.

What are you good at?

Today I want you to start to acknowledge what you're good at. And this might be easy if you're familiar with your strengths and you own and acknowledge them. On the other hand, it might be hard, because you don't believe you have many strengths. On a bad day, you might not believe you have any. If that sounds familiar, I get it. I've had those days and weeks, and I've also worked with clients who found it impossible to list their strengths, even though they were high achievers whom anyone from the outside would deem to be highly successful. First though, let me tell you a story. I'm a champion windsurfer. I got a bronze medal. Yes, actually. I mean, I know I may not look like it. Heck, I don't even feel like it, but in a box in a cupboard in my house is a medal with my name on it. Scottish Windsurfing Championships 1992, Women's Under 15s, bronze medal.

And I'm not even any good at windsurfing. Actually, let's pause there. Because there's been huge learning for me in this.

Throughout my adult life, I have rarely mentioned this achievement – usually only in the type of situations where I had to come up with 'two truths and a lie', and if I did ever tell the story, I would explain how windsurfing was in its infancy in Scotland when I was a teenager. Every Saturday, I used to go to a freezing loch in the Scottish Borders, squeeze myself into a wetsuit that never felt big enough and desperately try to learn something which seemed completely illogical. Each weekend I would persevere and enjoy the hot chocolate afterwards. So, when the Scottish championships were hosted at the same place, it wasn't even a question about whether or not I would enter. Have I mentioned my competitive nature before now?

To tell the truth, I don't actually remember the day of the championship itself. I don't know how well I surfed or what the weather conditions were. But somehow, I came third. A bronze medal. For me. I am the least athletic person I know, so this was some kind of a miracle. And on the day, I do remember being proud – I felt I had achieved something. Because of course I had. I was on the loch; I sailed and came third. It was an achievement, and one that nobody can take away from me.

But here's the thing. Ever since then, I have diminished that achievement. When I've told the story it's been in jest, joking about the fact that there were so few people windsurfing that I would have had to try to *not* get a medal. But that's not true. Out there in that wetsuit, I was showing that I had courage, that I was willing to be adventurous and try a new sport. I was demonstrating that I was willing to learn and had the tenacity to stick with it. And I also showed my competitive nature, among many other things. The medal shows a lot, and now that I've reflected on it further, I recognise the achievement for what it truly is. I won't joke about it again, because I now see it for what it represents.

I wonder where you are diminishing your achievements or not recognising what you are truly capable of?

What might become possible if you claimed your potential and your accomplishments?

We are going to do exactly that. Pick up a pen and paper now, or your journal, and start a list. What are you good at? Here are some categories to get you started:

- ➡ What are you good at in your job?
- ➡ What are you good at as a parent, if you have children?
- ➡ What makes you a good friend?
- ➡ What are you good at, at home?
- ➡ What are you good at in your community or as a citizen?
- ➡ What are you good at in taking care of yourself?
- ➡ What are you good at in your family?
- ➡ What's your hidden talent that nobody knows about?
- ➡ What would your best friend say are your strengths?
  (If you don't know, now is a good time to ask them!)
- ➡ What's one thing that people consistently say you're good at? (This might be your superpower by the way!)

I know how hard this can be, so be kind to yourself. Pour out what's in your head. Be wild and bold. Claim your brilliance! And if you need to ask people for help, ask friends, colleagues, former colleagues and maybe even your family members.

> Where are you diminishing your achievements?

Own the things you're good at, small and large, work and home. You have strengths and talents. It's time to recognise them so that we can build on them as you live through change.

What energises you?

Sometimes there are things that we're good at but they *drain* us. Often, they are things that we've done for a long time or done a lot of recently. And although we are still good at them, we get to a point where we've just basically had enough! It's important to recognise those things and to distinguish them from things that we're good at which energise us, particularly if you've not got a lot of energy. I want you to look back at the list of your strengths that you made in the previous section, and mark with a star the things you've listed which *energise* you. Mark with a minus sign the things that *drain* you. We're going to make sure that you maximise the things that energise you, and minimise the things that drain you as you live through change. Think of the strengths that energise you as rocket fuel. If you're good at something and it energises you, the more you do of it, the more you'll be energised and you'll be achieving success. That's got to be a good thing, whether you're living with change you've chosen or change that life has thrown at you.

As an example, I am really good at taking responsibility; I've done it pretty much my whole life – I pick up things and take responsibility for them, seeing them through to fruition, fixing things or making things happen. But when I do too much of it, over a longer period, I get to the stage where I've had enough. I start to become grumpy; I resent those around me for not taking responsibility; and then I know it's time to step back and let others take the reins. It's not that I lose my strength in this area, it's just that it no longer brings me energy. So, looking back at your list, pay attention to those things with a minus sign next to them – how can you minimise or moderate them so that others can take over and you can protect your energy? What can you ask someone to do today, that would give you even an ounce more energy? Because, of course, something that drains you, may well energise someone else. Take organising for example. It drains me, but my middle sister will always be energised by sorting things out, so asking her to help me with that is a good idea!

Summary

We've got started! You've begun the steps to clarify who you are, what your purpose is, what matters, your strengths and what energises you. I don't expect you to have answers to each of those fully captured. It's just a start. When clients work through these things in coaching, any one of these pieces can take weeks of exploration. The aim of this book is for you to get the whole picture, to start the untangling and have access to the resources to come back to over and over again as and when you want or need to. It's designed so you can access it in small pieces, and give yourself, the person who's here now, the space to discover more about yourself as you navigate your current change. What

> When we know differently, we choose differently

matters is that you keep working through it, that you take time to reflect and record those reflections and that your actions start to shift as a result. When we know differently, we choose differently.

Each section in this book will help you to know differently when you pick up a pen and start to untangle your thoughts, feelings and beliefs. So, pick up the pen now!

Journalling prompts

Take a minute now to capture what you're noticing about yourself:

- ➡ What's surprised you about this first step of clarifying?
- ➡ Are you surprised by how much you know or how much you feel is still unanswered?
- ➡ How does that feel?
- ➡ What's the piece you want to explore further just now?
- ➡ What's the piece that still feels too hard?
- ➡ What's the permission you need to give yourself to help you keep moving?

Chapter 3:
Connect

Introduction

Now that you've started to dig into who you are and started to get clarity, it's time to take a closer look at your change starting point. If you're enthusiastic about creating change, it can be easy to jump straight in and get started. I get it, I've been there and launched headfirst into something, only to realise partway through that it wasn't actually what I wanted. I even started a master's degree in neuroscience at the start of the pandemic which I soon stopped, after only completing the first module. If I'd taken the time to follow my own process, I would have realised faster, that what I wanted and needed was something to fill the time in lockdown, to give me a focus and to stimulate my mind. There were many ways I could have done that; I jumped into the first one that presented itself to me. I don't regret the choice – I learned some cool science stuff and was proud of my results for that first module – but it's not something I think I'll ever finish. My passion isn't in the sciences. This section is about connecting with ourselves and with our lives, so that in step three we can choose and move forward from there. If you're facing change that life has handed you, this piece around connecting might feel painful. Connecting to how you feel can be difficult, and it is an important part of coming to terms with what's happened. I know from personal experience that shutting down emotions can be a natural response and it does come back to bite you. If this feels beyond challenging, please be gentle with yourself and get professional help if you need it.

By the end of this section, you'll have discovered or confirmed what's here now and what your starting point is. You will have reflected on your story so far, at least the parts that are relevant. You'll also have identified how you feel, what you need, and what's getting in the way for you in the change you're facing now. Along the way I'll share stories from my life and from clients, and we'll also be building skills to help you with this and future change. Think of it as building the muscles you need to face change in the future, and doing it by living through the change that's here for you now.

What's here now?

The chances are that you are not expecting whatever change you are going through to fundamentally change you as a person. And the equally strong chances are, that it will. Because when we live through change – both the kind we choose and the kind life throws at us – we end up altered. Like rocks that sit in the bottom of a river, over time we are changed by our life experiences – rough edges are smoothed away; parts that stick out get knocked off; and, ultimately, we do become more rounded.

> Like rocks that sit in the bottom of a river, over time we are changed by our life experiences

Of course, with some kinds of change, it's much more immediate and much more obvious. When you go through a divorce or a job loss, you can feel like you have lost all sense of yourself, and you don't know where to start in building a new future. I remember when my marriage ended. I'd been with my then husband for seventeen years and we realised that the marriage was no longer serving either of us. It was a painful process, in fact one that lasted many, many months until we finally reached the conclusion that there was no forward path together. I was still completely devastated: the loss of the future I had envisaged for myself and our family; the sense of failure at not having managed to make our marriage work, and a complete confusion about who I was. We got together when I was eighteen and he was seventeen. I barely knew who I was without our relationship. Yes, I had a life, a career, friends and hobbies, but who was I really? Moving out of our home, I realised I'd never even spent

> I felt like I was made of Lego. All of the pieces had been taken apart, but I had lost the picture on the box

a weekend by myself, in my own home. It scared me. I didn't know how to be on my own. I didn't want to be on my own and face the feelings of failure. I was thirty-five and my marriage had ended. I needed to learn how to be on my own – fast. I was lonely. Or at least I would have been lonely, if I had only stopped long enough to feel it. I filled the time so the loneliness wouldn't catch me.

I remember talking to a trusted friend and I described it this way. I said I felt like I was made of Lego. All of the pieces had been taken apart, but I had lost the picture on the box. I didn't know who I was, and I didn't know what was possible or who I might become. Of course, that feeling didn't last forever – I found myself, and I created a new future for me and for my daughter and, ultimately, a new way of co-parenting with my ex-husband that, most of the time, has worked for both of us. But in that time of deep change, I lost sight of myself and my identity. And I'm talking about this now because I want you to know that it is okay if you feel like that. In fact, it's pretty much inevitable, particularly if you are facing change that you didn't choose or plan for but also if you are facing change that you did create. When we shift big stuff in our lives, it throws lots into the melting pot, including who we are and how we view ourselves. Maybe you are creating a big relationship change and it throws into question the way you see yourself in regard to loyalty. Or perhaps you're creating a career change that feels so significant that you no longer recognise yourself when you look in the mirror. If you've trained for something for years or even decades and then decide to move away from it, you might wonder what you're doing and what's changed inside you. I want you to know that it's all okay. You are you. You have the absolute right to change. What worked for you yesterday, might not work for you today, and you might end up reinventing yourself several times over in this game we call life. Whatever you choose now is also not forever. You can change again. And again. And again if you want to. Keep getting to know yourself. Look in the mirror and see who's here now. Get to know that person and get to love them. It's your closest friend and your greatest source of support – always there, after all. And, based on my own experience, when we change in big ways, we may not always notice until we get to the other side. So, take note of who's here now – maybe stick a photo of you in this book with a date on it, or write a few words about who you are now. You may want to come back to that in a few months, or even years, and be surprised by what you see. You are a living, transforming human. Notice the evolution.

What's your starting point?

You know, most people don't actually start their change at the beginning. Or at least, they don't realise that they are at the start, until they look back. Because most change that you choose begins with a whisper, a fragment of an idea. And most reactive change comes so fast out of nowhere that you don't even see it coming. So today we start by looking at where you are in your change. Are you at the very beginning, with only a glimmer of an idea? Do you find yourself daydreaming and wondering what might happen if you changed things a little – or a lot? Have you got a nagging sense that there is something different that you'd love to pursue? Or just a feeling that things aren't quite the way you'd like them to be? Late at night, are you aware of a bigger dream, if only you could get clarity on what it looks like?

Maybe you're clearer on what you want, have more sense of awareness of the change you'd like to bring to fruition, but you're not sure how? And maybe you're already starting to experiment with change, to take the steps to create your new future. Before you go too much further into this book, let's take a little moment or two today to be aware of your starting point. You picked this book up for a reason right now. You're reading these words because part of you wants or needs to change, and you recognise that there might be some things you can learn that will help you. So, here's my invitation to you: pause, take stock of where you are so that, as you move, progress and evolve, you can look back and notice how far you've come. The next section will help you to do that.

I once made a commitment to myself that I would do a hundred personal training sessions in the gym in one year. I knew I wanted to get fitter. I was frustrated by not making any progress at the gym. I know myself well enough to know that I needed a big challenge that scared me to get myself motivated. So a hundred PT sessions was the big challenge. It felt bigger than two sessions a week, even though the numbers are the same. And it definitely scared me. I felt the urge to run away, felt slightly overwhelmed by the size of the goal, but I also knew I had support from my personal trainer and that I had achieved big, scary things before. It took me a little longer than I had planned, but I did it. I gained incredible strength through my time working in that way, physical and mental, but I do also wish that I had taken a couple of moments at the start of the journey to capture who I was then, what I thought and believed, and what I was capable of physically and mentally. I knew I made progress, but by the end it was also hard to see that sometimes because I didn't have the 'before' data to show me where I started. I hadn't taken any photographs, so I didn't have any way to look back at the (lack of) definition of my muscles. I didn't write down what weights I was using, so I couldn't later easily see the progress I'd made. And I hadn't journalled specifically about how I felt in relation to my body, my strength, or the way I saw myself. Let's make sure we help you to capture the starting place for you, in whatever way feels most resonant, even before we begin to get clear on the change you want to create. Use some time today to get a sense of your beginning.

What's true for you now? Maybe you have a sense that your relationship needs to change, or that you want more fulfilment at work, or that you want to do something big. Perhaps life feels good, and you just have an inkling of an idea that won't seem to go away. You might see an opportunity that could lead to a business, there could be a course that keeps catching your eye, or even something that makes you just keep stopping and wondering 'what if I....'. You may also be feeling you don't like what's here. Living through reactive change, it's still helpful to capture what's here so that you can see how far you come in adapting and responding to change you don't choose.

Take some time to reflect on what your life is like now, the inside and the outside. In the 'Choose' chapter, we'll look at where the change fits. There's an activity which will help you to reflect on specific aspects of your life, how fulfilling they are and where you might want to make changes. We start by looking at the broader brushstrokes of your life just now. Give yourself permission to linger here, and then we'll go into more of the richness that captures how you are living and who you are now.

- Who are you now?
- What brings you joy and fulfilment in your life?
- What are you longing for?
- Who do you want to become?
- What do you appreciate about yourself now?

What's the story so far?

Today's content might have a few of you scratching your head and wondering why we might look at your life up until now. And let's be clear, I'm not talking about looking at the minutiae of every aspect of your life, which would probably take ages. This also isn't about looking at your past from a therapeutic angle, although it can be useful to work with a therapist if there is big stuff in your background which still feels like it has a significant and detrimental effect on you today.

We do this work of mapping your life to here to make sure that the change you make now builds on your life so far. You can relatively easily jump into creating any changes in your life, but if you don't have a sense of how your life so far has shaped the person sitting reading this book, you might find it hard to recognise and overcome any barriers to change as they arise. You may also find it tricky to get true clarity on what you want to change, and what's important about that.

I know from my own experience that looking back can sometimes be painful. There may be parts of our history that we would honestly rather gloss over and certainly not actively remind ourselves of. I didn't really want to go back and look at what happened when I lost my job, but it was important to help me understand what matters to me in my work and career. If I'd swept that under the carpet, I would have lost some of the rich wisdom that I could gather up from that time. Looking at the past helped me to create a better future. Identifying the patterns and themes of my previous experience, and reflecting on how I'd handled them, gave me different choices for how I handled things in the future. It wasn't easy. It was absolutely worth it. So please handle yourself with care and kindness as you work through these pages, and use today's reflection and action in a way that is sensitive to you and your needs, whilst also acknowledging that you do have a past. You have not just landed from another planet. You have existed before now, and your story shapes the thoughts, beliefs, feelings and dreams you have, in more ways than you can probably ever imagine. Let's harness that in a positive way, so that the future you create from this moment onwards is the life of your dreams. We can paint a new future. We can write a new ending. And it's built on the foundations you already have.

> Your story shapes the thoughts, beliefs, feelings and dreams you have

I'd like you to imagine that you have got a brilliant new pair of glasses. They've got a magic quality to them. Putting these glasses on means that you can look at any part of your life up until now with total clarity, absolute compassion and see what impact that past has on you today. The glasses are only for you, so you can be safe in the knowledge that nobody else can put them on. You can also be reassured that they actually do allow you to look back at your past self without judgement. These glasses are incapable of showing you any blame towards yourself. They aren't rose-tinted; they are simply here to show you your own past without any of the usual self-criticism that so many of us carry around with us all of the time.

So, whenever you're ready, pop the glasses on and let's look back at your life so far, for the sake of understanding the role it might play in creating your future.

You can choose how you'd like to look at your past. Perhaps you'd like to look at what you've learned. Or to look at the key people in your life and the gifts that they've given you. Or maybe even how you've grown. I'm sure you all remember those height charts that showed us how we kept getting taller as kids. You could use these glasses to look at what you knew and were aware of at key milestones in your life and to notice how you have evolved. Perhaps the change you're longing for is more work-related, so you could use these glasses to look at the work aspects of your life, the roles you've had up until now, the skills you've gained through them, and the ways in which those roles have allowed you to live in alignment with your values. If you're dreaming of launching a new business, or starting a new hobby, maybe look back at the key times at which you were doing or learning something new. Take whichever approach is going to serve you most and, of course, you can always look at your life from different angles and perspectives – it's your choice. You might notice that you are drawn to the stressful, difficult or painful moments in your life. That's okay, just make a note of them and ask yourself some of the following, to guide your mind towards the bigger picture:

- ➤ What relationships have been significant?
- ➤ What have been your most memorable moments?
- ➤ When have you been your absolute best self?
- ➤ What's been the biggest learning in your life so far?
- ➤ What would your closest friends and supporters say?

At various points in my life, I've looked at different parts of my story so far. Each time I find myself becoming more compassionate towards myself and less likely to judge myself for the choices I've made or the things that I've done before. I've looked at the decisions I've made, how relationships have worked and where they've failed. I've reviewed work situations and choices along the way. There is much more on self-compassion and self-care in the 'Untanglers' section because I see the challenges of self-judgement and self-criticism every day in my work with clients, and it actually pains me to see how often we beat ourselves up or treat ourselves in ways that we would never dream of inflicting on others. So, try to notice if some of that comes up for you; turn the corner of the page at the start of Chapter 8 and know that you will learn the skills to help you be kind to yourself as part of creating your change.

Take some time to capture what you notice and become aware of. You might want to create a timeline showing the key milestones and what was happening for you then. Or to compile a series of snapshots that tell the story of you over the course of your life so far. Perhaps you could make a collage of words that consolidate how you have felt at different times. Clients have also made mood boards for different stages of their lives, for example, each decade or key chapters in their story. Or you can keep it simple and make some lists and bullet points of what you start to recognise as you look back. Whatever comes into your mind may well be relevant, so trust yourself and note it down, so that we can come back to it later.

How do you feel and what do you need?

One of the absolutely vital skills we train for when we work with leaders and leadership teams is the ability to notice how we feel and put words to it. It seems such a basic thing, but it's not something that always comes easily to people. We are not often encouraged to say how we actually feel. If someone asks how you are, it seems easier to give a superficial answer. Many leaders we work with struggle to answer beyond 'happy', 'sad' and 'pissed off'. This might be something you find challenging too, so I want to help you build this new muscle. When you stop and think about how you feel, you might find it hard to either identify it or to give it an accurate label. The answer 'fine' is not going to help you very much.

There's a body of work called non-violent communication by American psychologist Marshall Rosenberg, which is based on the idea that how we feel and what we need are closely linked, and how we communicate that matters. A lot of behaviours that can be challenging to deal with, in ourselves and in others, often come from the fact that

> We are not often encouraged to say how we actually feel

we struggle to know what we're feeling or what we need. For me, it's an ongoing learning process, and I know the difference it can make in my whole life, particularly when going through change. To be able to notice that I'm feeling overwhelmed or apprehensive, or even thankful, then gives me a new set of doorways to start to recognise what I need. I also notice that I need to be careful to recognise the subtleties of how I'm feeling and to notice that I can feel more than one thing at once. When I started my business, and many times since then, I've felt anxious about the possibility of the business failing, and I've also felt a nervous excitement about the possibility of it being wildly successful. When I pay attention to how I feel, I can then start to explore what I need. If I'm feeling overwhelmed, I may need to talk with a friend or take a short break. If I'm feeling anxious, I might need to remind myself that there is always more than one way forward. And if I'm feeling nervous excitement or anticipation, I might need some deep breaths to remind me to slow down and stay in the present moment. If you want more help with identifying the range of emotions, visit my website for a downloadable resource.

It can be helpful to simply take two minutes in the morning when you start your day to notice how you feel and what you need. Try to tie that practice to another habit you already have, like brushing your teeth or waiting for the kettle to boil for the first time in the morning. This is called habit stacking or tethering and you might have come across it in the bestselling book *Atomic Habits* by James Clear. Reflecting on how we feel and what we need can also be a great chance to write yourself a permission slip. Take a sticky note, or even a piece of paper, and write at the top of it 'I give myself permission to...' and then write what it is that you need. This gives you the space and creates the possibility that you can then turn into reality. I learned this technique from Dr Brené Brown and, when I first met her in London to train as a facilitator of *The Daring Way*, her denim jacket pockets were full of permission slips. Learning to be a facilitator of her courage-building programme, this was one of many rich resources which I use with clients regularly. It's such a simple tool, and it can be surprisingly effective, because it encourages you to slow down and connect with how you're feeling, what you need, and then to actually write that down.

So today, right now, how are you feeling, and what do you need?

What's getting in the way?

The last piece of connecting with what's here for you now is to discover what's getting in the way. Chapters 5 and 8 have more detailed sections on how to cope with the different feelings that change brings up which you can dip into when you need to. For now, we're going to make sure we identify any of the barriers to change that you're currently experiencing. When we work with clients, it often surprises them that we take time to pay attention to what's getting in the way. The thing that catches people out is the simplicity of some of these barriers to change and also the ways in which they don't always seem related to the change that's in front of them.

I remember working with a leader in a technology company. They were creating big changes in the way the organisation was structured, how people worked together and the overall culture. They knew what they needed to do, and they kept stalling. We took time to step back and look at what was getting in the way, and in one particularly poignant conversation, tears came to their eyes, and they said in a half-whisper, 'I just don't want them to hate me.' This one fear stopped this leader – and the whole organisation – in their tracks. The deep-seated human desire to be liked and appreciated was holding back the change. We worked with that concern, and we started to look at how likely that was, what was important about it and who the leader had that they could count on. Slowly, the person was able to start to engage with the change. Before long, they realised that if they acted in integrity, in line with their values, and they reached out to people who could support them, they were able to keep going, and to trust they were doing the right thing. Whilst nobody wants to be hated, the fear of it doesn't need to stop you from doing what needs to be done, with integrity. It seems simple; it can be transformative.

So, take time just now to pause and connect with what's stopping you as you move into this change.

- I'm holding back because...
- If I go ahead with this change people will think...
- I'm scared that...
- My worst nightmare would be...

What are you noticing? You might already be able to see that these things seem real and powerful, and when you step back a bit, it could be more obvious that they're not actually very likely to happen. Usually when my team and I work with people, and ask them what the risk is if they change, they say they're worried that they won't be liked. When we ask what the risk of that is, they say they'll be passed over for promotion. When we ask what the risk of that is, they say they'll eventually lose their jobs. When we ask what the risk of that is, they say they'll become homeless. Eventually, if you follow this path, human beings worry about dying on their own and nobody coming to their funeral. And the reality is that this is a very, very unlikely outcome from you creating a small change, or even a big change, in your life. While it seems obvious to our logical mind, our emotional response is often driven by our sub-conscious mind and until we look at these things directly by asking these questions, we don't realise the emotions that are driving our actions. These deep-seated human fears are the ones that stop us all and hold us back. You are not alone. It's why I've written Chapters 5 and 8. You'll get the tools to handle all the key feelings that happen throughout change and resources to help you overcome the barriers. I remember watching Nadia Hussain, who won *The Great British Bake Off* in 2015, as she accepted the trophy. Scarlet and I watched those programmes avidly for many years, and this particular series was inspirational. Watching Nadia as she battled her own lack of self-confidence and seeing the palpable growth in her at the end of the series was emotional, and touched Scarlet and me. I often think of the words she used in her acceptance speech, spoken from the heart and with her feelings right on the surface:

I'm never gonna put boundaries on myself ever again. I'm never gonna say I can't do it. I'm never gonna say "maybe". I'm never gonna say "I don't think I can". I can. And I will.

British Baker Nadia Hussain, *The Great British Bake Off*, 2015

The reality, of course, is that we do put boundaries on ourselves. We absolutely do tell ourselves we can't, and we often say 'maybe' or that we 'think' we can. The trick is to notice it when it's happening. Before those limiting beliefs keep us from living the life we want to live, we need to stop and take action to keep them where they belong and to step forward regardless. You can. And you will.

For now, what are one or two sentences you want to write down that will remind you that these worst-case scenarios are highly unlikely? What's the reality?

- I am...
- I can...
- And I will...

Summary

This chapter has given you the prompts and support to reflect on:

- What's here now?
- What's your starting point?
- What's the story so far?
- How do you feel and what do you need?
- What's getting in the way?

As you work through these sections, you're pulling apart the threads that were tangled so that you can start to weave something new. You may choose to create change, you may not. And yet here you are, picking up the knotted cords and gently teasing them apart so that your future can become a reality. It takes courage. It's not easy. It is absolutely worth it. Take a minute to just reflect on the fact that you're in this, and you are being intentional about the life you are living. That's a gift to yourself and it's a gift to those around you. The more you show up and live your life authentically and with courage, the more you inspire and support others to do the same. So, from me to you, thank you. Keep going.

Journalling prompts

Looking around at your life just now, take time to capture and consolidate the themes that you are aware of:

- What have the positive threads in your life been so far?
- What are some of the current themes?
- If your life was a film, what would have been the story up until now and what's the current scene?
- What might the soundtrack be?
- What's most important to you right now?

Chapter 4:
Choose

Introduction

The third step in untangling your path is to choose. Now is the time to start to reflect on what you want. In this chapter, we'll get much more understanding of what you want, where it fits with your life, what's the ideal, what's important about the change and, vitally, who's on your support team and is there to help you. By the time we get to the end of this chapter, you will have chosen the threads that are going to be part of this next stage of your life. And you'll be starting to see how they could fit together.

This step is big. It's the point where things start to become more real for change you've chosen, and can involve some painful acceptance for change you've not. So, give yourself the space you need to take your time with these sections, and if you need help with some of the feelings that come up, have a look at Chapter 8.

What do you want?

Let's start by exploring what you want. What you really want. The thing or things that you might not even have truly realised or acknowledged to yourself. This will probably include the initial change that brought you to pick up this book, but it might also surprise you to discover other things that you actually dream of.

We often have hidden desires that we either choose not to listen to, or we have learned to tune out, in order to get through our day-to-day lives. I mean the thing that gives you butterflies and possibly even a sense of 'yeah, but I couldn't possibly....'. One for me, is that I would love to play the piano well. I know that I want to have that ability. I want to be able to sit down and play. I tried when I was younger. My grandpa gave us a piano when I was about fourteen. He knew I wanted to learn but that we couldn't afford one. I wanted to study music when I was older. So, he found a beaten-up old piano for me to learn on. It wasn't great, but it was enough. I could practise and pass the exams I needed. I've just always wanted to get better and to be able to play music that I love for pleasure. But I drown the idea out most days because I tell myself it would take too much practice, that I don't have the time and I'd probably suck at it anyway. Some of those things may be true, but if I don't ever even listen to the desire, I guess I'll never find out. It might be time for me to start to listen to that whisper. What might be possible if I chose to follow that dream? Playing the piano might build my confidence; it might inspire my family; it might enable me to bring joy to others. There are endless possibilities.

> We often have hidden desires that we either choose not to listen to, or we have learned to tune out

So perhaps there is some musical fantasy in your mind, or a glimmer of an idea about living somewhere different or doing something in your community. Today is the day when we start to slow down, listen and capture your dreams on paper. We'll take time to connect with what you genuinely want. It's a beginning and you may want to repeat this exercise many times over. As with all things relating to change, it starts with the first step.

It's a remarkable thing that, as human beings, we don't usually give ourselves time to think about what we really want. We might give it a fleeting thought at key times in our lives – some of us might also set intentions at the start of each year or when we start a new job – but we rarely stop and think about what we want from this one human existence we have. Mary Oliver asks the question in her poem *The Summer Day*:

Tell me, what is it you plan to do

With your one wild and precious life?

I wonder how you feel when you read those lines? Maybe go back and read them again? I'll wait. Do you feel a chill run over your body or a rush of excitement? Perhaps a bit of nausea and a sense of regret? Or a spark of adrenaline as you begin to open up to all that is possible? As with everything in this book, there is no right answer. You will feel what you feel, and this is just the very beginning.

You might be excited to get stuck into the exercises, or you might feel a bit daunted or tempted to skip these pages and move on to the next stage. Whatever you feel is okay, just notice it, thank yourself for all the creative stories you're making up in your mind and keep reading.

I realise that this might be something you haven't thought about before, or it might be something you actively resist. Maybe you've been on the same path since you were at school, following the route that someone else laid out for you. Perhaps you've tried to carve your own way before, and it didn't go so well. It can be scary to look at the future, particularly if you've had a history of things not turning out the way you wanted them to, or hoped they would. To stop and think about what you really, truly want can sometimes feel like you're setting yourself up for disappointment – what if you let yourself acknowledge what you want and then it doesn't happen? What if you start to pay attention to some of the big dreams you have and then you stall and they stall too? I get it. It takes courage to listen to your inner wisdom, the part of you that still dares to dream, the part of you that wants to make a different future. And yet, it can be so liberating and bring you such possibility to just give yourself the gift of time and space to listen to your heart's desire. To allow yourself to pause, even for ten minutes, and pay attention to what you want.

Growing up I was often told 'I want doesn't get'. It was a way to teach my sisters and me to have manners and ask nicely for things. But it doesn't allow you to listen to your own inner wanting. In fact, it can stop you from paying attention to what you want, what you long for and what you truly desire. It's still a phrase and a belief that sometimes trips me up. If I'm not careful I can start to believe that it's true. Actually, I've learned it's sometimes completely false. The received wisdom that people who want things don't get them just isn't true. In fact, when we acknowledge and articulate what we want, we create the potential for it to become a reality. It's taken me decades to learn to listen to what I want and to say it out loud. I have to work at it. Laura Whitworth, one of the co-founders of Co-Active Coaching said '**I get to want what I want. I get to, I just get to. I get to ask for what I want. I get to. I just get to. And I'm willing to negotiate the difference**'. This transformed my thinking about listening to what I want and need, and then to negotiate the difference between what I want and need, and what's possible given what other people also want and need. I'm forever grateful to Helen House for sharing it with me.

For today I'd like you to put that parenting quip to one side, and I give you full permission to want whatever you want to. And let's be clear – some of the things you want might be specific, tangible things that you want to have. You might want to have strawberry ice cream for dinner. You might want to have shoes that don't rub. You might want to have a comfy sofa with coordinating scatter cushions or even a new pet. Those are all great things. Write them down if that's what comes up for you in the activity. And you might also have bigger things that you want – like a house in the country or a job that fills you with joy and fulfilment. You might also have things that you want to do, experiences you'd like to live, missions you'd like to accomplish, impact that you'd like to have in your community or things that you'd just like to be the case when they perhaps aren't right now. You might want to know that your children will have a financially secure future. You might want there to be an end to homelessness. You might want all kinds of things. Write them all down, every single one. Whatever comes up when you do this activity is okay. Let yourself capture your ideas on paper, no judgement, just let the words flow. For now, you're just writing words on a page. So free yourself up to listen to what you want, and write down all the things. Have fun!

What do you want (Exercise)

Today's exercise is one that we've used in Firefly, the business I created, with individual leaders and also with teams, to help them look at the much bigger picture of what they want. If you like it, and it works for you, you can ask yourself all kinds of questions, each starting with 'what do you want?'. You can look far, far into the future as well as close up. It's an activity I learned from an inspirational mentor called Dave Ellis, which I've adapted for this purpose. It helps you to be clear on what you want and to become more creative in making that a reality. As Barnet Bain says in his treasury of creative exercises: *The Book of Being and Doing*, 'Your whole life is a creative act'.

You will need a pen, a timer and lots of bits of paper you can write on – index cards are ideal; sticky notes can work (though they tend to get stuck to each other); or cut up some bits of coloured paper and use those.

For this activity you're going to settle in, get comfy and let your subconscious start to tell you what you want. It might help to take a few deep breaths to settle yourself before you start.

Set a timer for sixty seconds for each question, and write as many answers as your pen will let you write; just keep writing until the timer stops. It's helpful if you can write one idea or response per piece of paper or index card so that, later, you can filter them, sort them or build on them further. You'll end up with lots of bits of paper, and that's great!

So, set your timer for the first minute and let's get started with the first question (you can even read the question aloud to yourself – unless you're on a commuter train or in your work canteen at lunchtime!): What do you want twenty years from now?

Now, for sixty seconds, write down everything that comes into your mind.

Great work! Now, set the timer for another sixty seconds and ask the following question: What do you want ten years from now?

Keep writing for the full time, even if you end up duplicating your answers – that in itself is telling you something.

Now repeat the process for the following questions, each for one minute:

➤ What do you want five years from now?

- What do you want a year from now?
- What do you want six months from now?
- What do you want that's just for you?
- What do you want for your family and those you love?
- What do you want for your community?
- What do you want for your country?
- What do you want for humanity?

What a lot of ideas! Now you can no longer say that you don't know what you want. I'm willing to bet that there are still more ideas inside you that we've not yet tapped into. Perhaps group them into things you want to have, do and be. Have a look at what you've written; maybe journal a bit in the coming days about what things you noticed, and then save these cards somewhere safe so that we can come back to them in the future.

Where does this fit into your life?

Now let's look at how the change you long for fits into your wider life.

Sometimes we are tempted to dive straight into creating the change we want to achieve. And there's nothing hugely wrong about that. In fact, there are times when the impetus grabs you by the hand and you simply have to make the move. The idea won't wait; the urge is too great – it's time! If it feels like that is where you are right now, keep going! Perhaps mark the corner of this page as one to come back to when the full-throttle-can't-wait-a-minute sensation

When we do jump straight in, we don't take the time to think about how the change we want to create fits with the rest of our lives eases a little. You might be glad you did, because I have witnessed in both my own life and those of others, that sometimes when we do jump straight in, we don't take the time to think about how the change we want to create fits with the rest of our lives. We don't linger long enough to contemplate if the knock-on impact in the other aspects of our lives is truly what we want or how we can make sure that it is. We can then end up in a clean-up operation when the dust settles from the initial shift in our lives.

I know - I've done it before. I ended up in a job that I absolutely hated for a while. I leapt before I looked. On the surface it seemed like a good opportunity, but the reality was completely different. And with the benefit of hindsight, some of the warning signs were there in advance, but I didn't have time to see them, let alone ignore them. I jumped straight in, took the job and it took me almost two years to dig myself out of it. I wish I'd slowed down a little and taken a bit more time to look at the impact on my home life, my parenting and, ultimately, my mental wellbeing. It might have given me signs towards a different choice. And yes, I learned from it, and it's part of the overall path of my life, so I won't beat myself up for it. I just recognise that sometimes we can take a different turning, if we stop and think about the wider impacts ahead of making those steps. In Chapter 6 we will look at what we learn from change. Of course, there are other times when I've taken a leap and it has worked out. I'm also not for a minute suggesting that we can predict every potential outcome from a change – indeed there wouldn't be much fun in that, as we would lose the magic that can occur precisely because we don't know what will happen. What I'm encouraging and promoting is that you take a little time to look at the bigger picture at this early stage. Go in with your eyes open. In some cases, this will completely and utterly validate that the change you are facing is going to have fantastic wider effects. In others it can help you realise that there are things that you might want to give your attention to, in order to mitigate any detrimental effect. And in other cases, you might stumble across something that will stop you short and make you realise that the change you thought you wanted is actually not what matters most to you. You may even end up following a different path.

For today, I'd like to invite you to take that pause. To stop, draw breath and think about how this change you long to create fits with the bigger picture. In the coming pages, I will give you some specific tools you can use to do just that. Let's dream big. Dare to look far into the future. Depending on where you are right now, you might want to think far ahead in terms of five years, ten years, even twenty years. You'll know the timeline that feels right for you – trust your instinct and imagine yourself there. Think about what your life might be like by then, who you might be surrounded by, what your priorities might be and what stage of life you'll be in. Notice how you feel. Notice what brings you joy. Notice the things that matter and the things that don't. Once you have a good sense of how life might be, let's look back at the place you are in now. Have a look at the change you're facing and ask yourself the following questions:

- What's the story you want to be able to tell about this time of change?
- What do you want to feel most proud of?
- What challenges do you want to have overcome?
- How did the change alter your priorities?

When I work with clients, I often invite them to look far into the future, typically five or ten years, sometimes more. We don't just do this for the perhaps obvious reason – to look at what changes they want to make – we also do it because I ask them to look back at the place they are in now and think about how they want to have handled the current situation. There's something quite magical about taking yourself into the future. I'm not sure I totally understand how, or why, it happens, but when you do take your mind forward, you tap into your values much more clearly than you are often able to in the here and now. So, give yourself the gift of that insight today and capture what comes up for you. Then think about what needs to change about your mission to make those things true. Is your mission still fully resonant? How do you feel now about the change in front of you?

It's possible this felt difficult. Perhaps you might have felt a sense of loss – or some judgement – of yourself or others. You might want to come back to this in the future as you work further through the change. Try not to label those things as 'good' or 'bad'; just notice them and realise that this is all here too. I love the following Taoist parable which illustrates that we may not always know what is good and what is bad for us, even though it can be tempting to label things in this way. See what happens if you can stay open a little to the possibility that things are not always as they seem.

Who Knows What Is Good and What Is Bad?

A Parable

When an old farmer's stallion won a prize at a country show, his neighbour called round to congratulate him, but the old farmer said, 'Who knows what is good and what is bad?'

The next day some thieves came and stole the valuable animal. When the neighbour came to commiserate with him, the old man replied, 'Who knows what is good and what is bad?'

A few days later the spirited stallion escaped from the thieves and joined a herd of wild mares, leading them back to the farm. The neighbour called in to share the farmer's joy, but the farmer responded, 'Who knows what is good and what is bad?'

The following day, while trying to break in one of the mares, the farmer's son got thrown and fractured his leg. The neighbour called to share the farmer's sorrow, but the old man's attitude remained the same as before.

The following week the army passed by, forcibly conscripting soldiers for the war, but they did not take the farmer's son because he couldn't walk. And the neighbour thought to himself, who knows what is good and what is bad? *realising that the old farmer must be a Taoist sage.*

(Taoist parable, original source unknown, this version taken from course materials for ORSC created by www.CRRglobal.com)

What's the ideal?

Now we're going to look at your life as it is now and as you'd like it to be. This is another way to help you get even more clarity about what matters to you, and how your change is going to help you live a more fulfilling life. Imagine if you were thriving in all aspects of your life. What would that be like? What would you be doing or not doing? Who might be with you in your life, and how would you be in those relationships? Let's explore what matters to you in different slices of your life.

Working with clients who have specific coaching goals, it would be all too easy to focus on one goal and not look at how it related to the rest of their lives, or indeed how it could benefit them in other ways. Take an example of a client who wants to complete an Ironman. Lorna was a mum of two children; she had a full-time job, but she also wanted to complete an Ironman triathlon. (This is definitely not a challenge for me to undertake – you have to swim

2.4 miles, cycle 112 miles and then run a marathon – it's a feat of endurance, to say the least!) It would be tempting to dive straight into the training for that, without looking at how it could impact the relationships with her children or husband, what might be needed from a work point of view to support her endeavours, or what else might need to change. So, we used a tool called the wheel of life to explore the other aspects that might need to be considered before she jumped into the training, and I promise it wasn't a source of procrastination! What she discovered was that the triathlon was important, and she wanted to make sure she spent time with her family, which she decided to prioritise at the weekends. She's gone on to complete several endurance events and been able to involve her family and include them in her plans. She didn't have to juggle all the balls, just the ones that wouldn't bounce.

You'll need a piece of paper or your journal to draw your own wheel of life, or you could use the notes pages at the end of this chapter. Definitely don't let a lack of paper be the thing that stops you from this reflection and from identifying what you need to refine about your change as a result. The Untangled Journal has a copy of the wheel of life for you to use.

Start by drawing a large circle so that the whole page is almost filled. Then divide the circle into segments so that it looks like a wheel. The easiest way to do this is to draw a line that cuts your circle in half, top to bottom, then draw a line across the middle from left to right so that you have quarters. Then divide each quarter into halves from the outside edge of the circle to the middle of the circle so that you end up with eight wedges or segments. (Hopefully you do now have something that looks like that, or at least roughly!).

We're going to label each segment of the circle with an aspect of your life. You can choose whatever segment labels work for you, just make sure that you are covering your whole life and that they feel resonant. Here are some suggestions for the segments:

- Financial
- Community
- Spiritual
- Romance/life partner
- Professional
- Fun
- Family
- Leisure
- Physical health
- Mental health
- Physical environment
- Personal growth

Now I'd like you to imagine that each segment represents how fulfilling that aspect of your life is. If the segment was totally unfulfilling right now, you'd colour none of it in, or maybe just the very tiniest piece, starting from the centre of the circle. If it was totally fulfilling, you'd colour the whole segment in, and if only half-fulfilling, you'd only have half of that segment coloured in. This doesn't have to be precise, but I'd like you to colour in each segment to show how fulfilling your life is now. (I'll wait while you dig out some coloured pens or just use the one you have nearest to you.)

Once you've done the colouring in, what do you notice? What's the thing that strikes you? Are there pieces that are fulfilling and others not at all? Or is the whole wheel pretty balanced at a particular level? Take a few minutes to notice what you're realising about your current life. And then, make notes on what it would take to make each segment a ten out of ten, fully coloured in, vibrant life. Each of those things can be a source of change, a prompt – small or large – to shift something in your life. And you might also be starting to realise that some of these changes can be the tiniest of tweaks. You don't have to make giant sweeping changes. In fact, in Chapter 5 I'm going to give you several strategies for making change more manageable. The things you've identified in today's work could be the springboard for lasting change. So, give yourself a virtual high five and file this somewhere safe – we're going to come back to it in the coming days, and use it to see how you can make changes to bring yourself more joy.

What's important about the change?

Simon Sinek talks about finding your 'why' and starting from there. In training to be coaches, we're often told to avoid using questions that start with 'why', because it can lead people to become defensive. But the reason for anything is important. Think of that incredible (okay, annoying) stage kids go through when they ask 'why' about everything and anything. I remember that stage vividly with my own daughter Scarlet, who basically realised that she could control the conversation if she just kept asking 'why?'. Over and over, whatever I said, she would ask 'why?', and there seemed to be no answer that would satisfy her. I often used to sigh in exasperation because there seemed to be no way out of the conversation. Was she learning? Yes. Was she also driving me crazy? Undoubtedly, also yes! Partly, I think kids do this because they've realised that if they ask 'why', they can keep adults talking literally forever. And I also think it's because it's a vital stage of development in understanding the reason for things, the way things connect and the way kids make sense of the world in a different way.

It can be so easy to step into facing change and not do so in a way that is anchored in purpose. To not understand how it connects and how it makes sense in our world. We've already looked at what you want and at how it fits with the rest of your life. Now is the time to look at what's important to you about this change. Why does it matter to you? It might be easy to assume that you know that, particularly in a big life change that you've been dreaming of for ages, or because it's something you've not chosen, like the loss of a job or the ending of a significant relationship. And it can be easy to overlook that or to get lost along the way. Part of what we're doing at this stage is setting out coordinates, mapping the key aspects of change. This way, when things get difficult or you doubt yourself, you can come back to the place you started and remind yourself what was important to you about this thing in the first place. I find it easy enough to lose my glasses or my car keys, let alone my rationale for something, so let's use some time to get that clear and captured for future reference. In their latest book *The Third Paradigm,* Ivan Misner, Dawa Phillips and Heidi Giusto highlight the need for the clarity and commitment to what matters as 'Hold the vision, not the obstacles'.

For change that chooses you, it might also seem a bit superfluous to think about why the change matters to you, but it comes back to what I said earlier about you being able to choose how you respond. What matters to you now in how you handle this change *is* important. If you have just been dealt a massive blow to your health, you might want to choose to handle it in small, day-at-a-time pieces, or you might want to use it as a catalyst for much bigger change. If you have had a close bereavement, you might want to use this as a time to connect more closely with other loved ones, to redefine your own priorities, or you might just want to use it to appreciate the tiny things in life every day. What matters to you about this change will guide you in your actions and reactions. It will form part of the framework for this change, and it could shape your future forever. Surely that's worth a bit of time?

So, today I'm going to invite you to go for a short walk, get yourself outside and listen to what your heart and soul have to say about why this change matters. The answer to this question doesn't come from a book. You can't actually think it into existence. But deep down inside, you know, with clarity and conviction, even though it might be scary. You truly know what matters to you about this change. Why is it important to you? What's the core of this change? Who are you going to become through this? What's the nature of this evolution of you?

> Listen to what your heart and soul have to say about why this change matters

When you come back from your stroll, find a way to capture your awareness in a way that works for you. You might take photographs and make a collage, write a few notes or make a playlist that you can come back to. Find a way that's tangible so that you can return to your 'why' when you need to.

Who's on your support team?

I imagine there have been times in your life when you have longed to be on an island, all by yourself, with nobody making any demands or requests of you. Perhaps only accompanied by someone who could bring you a nice cool, refreshing drink. But you are not actually an island – you are not disconnected from everyone and everything. And that matters when you're facing change in your life, because you will need other people to support you and be there for you as you face the unknown of what's ahead. You might find that hard to accept. You may resist the very notion that you need to lean on others. Quite possibly you might have created elaborate ways and means to be independent, to carry on by yourself, to potentially even offer lots of support to others, but be unwilling or unable to accept help yourself. We will come back to why 'help' is not a bad four-letter word in the future.

For now, though, let's start to think about who is in your support team. Brené Brown calls this your square squad: the people whose opinions and views truly matter to you. She suggests that the list of these people is so small that you can fit their names into a square that's only one inch by one inch. And that can stop us short when we think about all the other people whose opinions we bend ourselves out of shape for. Perhaps you worry about what your neighbours will think of your relationship ending, or the other parents at the school gate, or even your colleagues if you announce your resignation? Do their opinions honestly matter? In five years' time, will you remember and care what they said or thought about the choices that you made? I have spent far more hours than I care to add up, worrying about what other people will think. I've lost sleep concerned about how I would be judged or even condemned for the decisions I've made and the things that I've done. And on one hand that's perfectly normal. We are naturally community- and society-oriented. Most people want to be liked, or at very least accepted, by other human beings. We don't want to be cast out, left to live alone on a remote hillside with only sheep for our nearest companions, though there are times when that sounds like heaven on earth. Even people who are more introverted, and gain their energy from being alone, want to be connected. We want to feel valued; we want to be loved. And we tell ourselves (and sadly we tell our kids) that to fit in, to be acceptable to others, we have to be independent and to act in socially acceptable ways.

So, when we face change, we either stress and strain with concern about what *all* the others will think or how they will react. Or we go the other way – we retreat entirely into ourselves, tell ourselves that nobody's opinions matter, and we can do whatever the heck we like. In reality, of course, there is a middle way. And it's where it helps to identify whose opinions do actually matter to you, and also who is there to support you. By which I don't mean just blindly agreeing with you, and telling you that you can do anything you want, with no consequence. And I also don't mean people whose roles mean that they should support you, even if the reality looks quite different. I mean the people who, when faced with you and your future, will handle it with care, compassion and concern, but will also bring excitement, exhilaration and empowerment. The small, hand-picked support team that you have brought into your life because they 100% have your back. These people will show up for you in the middle of the night. They will answer your calls when you are lost and confused. They will hold your hand and tell you that you're right – you have messed up, and it is all going to be okay somehow, just as soon as the two of you have a cup of tea and can work out what's first in the rescue mission. These are the people who want you to succeed, who recognise that you need to be bold and brave, and take risks to face change and who are cheering you on all the way. They are also the people who will stand by your side as you let go of your losses, grieve the endings of previous chapters and look at the paths you don't want to take. These are your people. And, though you won't like it, and it will hurt, your people will change over time too. You might be incredibly fortunate and have people on your support team who are there for you your whole life, perhaps a friend from school, a sibling or a dear neighbour. And the rest will come and go throughout your life. We are rarely static in relationships and, as we change and evolve, we need different allies in our path through life.

So, it's vital to really take stock of who is in your crew now. Who are the people whom you will look towards as you work through this change? Who are the ones you choose and those who have chosen you? The chances are they are not far away. You've probably been in contact with them lately. They may know they are in your team, or you may need to invite them. Look left and right. Check your recent contacts in your phone. Or simply be still for a minute or two and think about who you want to have around you in this time. And if you are recently bereaved and have lost someone who was in your support team, be exquisitely gentle with yourself. The loss of anyone close will always impact you profoundly, and the loss of someone who has been your support through change can be even more acute. Tend to your heart and lean into the gifts they gave you in previous change. It will feel like they are irreplaceable. They are. And there is space for a different type of support from beyond the end of their human existence.

My mum was, at various points in my life, a member of my support crew. She believed in my abilities and was able to pick me up and dust me down when I doubted them. When my marriage ended, on one fateful night, I showed up at my parents' house. In a rare show of vulnerability, I collapsed, sobbing into her arms, and said, 'I can't do this.' Holding my shoulders, she pulled me up to my feet and simply said, 'You can. And you will.' Losing her while I was working on this book felt, in so many ways, like a gaping chasm that could never be filled. It won't be; it hasn't been. And, at the same time, my human need for support and connection saw me reach out to others who had not been as close in my life and draw them nearer to me. Instinctively, I recognised the need for support and connection, even when I wasn't able to articulate that to myself. I also know that Mum is with me, guiding these words, and all that she instilled in me, in the time she was alive, is inside me now and always will be.

So, take a moment now and write the names or initials of those who are in your support team. Notice if it feels hard. Think about who would want to be on that list. Who would be there for you and champion you across the finish line? Your crew can be tiny; it should definitely be a very select group. Because these are the people who *do* matter, not those who you think *should* matter. These are your clan. You might want to tell them, to make it explicit. Or you might want to just know, and start to look to them for support a little more.

Summary

This third step of choosing is where the reality starts to reveal itself. You now have much greater clarity about what you want, where it fits, what's the ideal, what's important about the change and who's on your support team.

It won't be perfect; you won't have all the answers. It's going to be messy; and there are likely still pieces to untangle and tease apart over the coming weeks, months and possibly years. And yet, you have done so much now to help you move forward with intentionality and a new perspective. You can take the steps into your own future. You will make different choices and take different actions. And you'll be living your life in a way that's more resonant and real for you. Take a deep breath – you're weaving the fabric of your life, one thread at a time.

You've done so much work – let's take a little bit of space to consolidate what's here for you now. Parts of it will still be a work in progress – that's called life. It's not meant to be perfect or finished, even when you draw your last breath. What matters is being conscious and intentional, choosing for now, so let's make sure you can see the choices you are making and what matters to you at this time.

- ➤ What's the change you want or need to make in your life?
- ➤ What's the bigger picture for that change that feels significant now?
- ➤ What themes in your life is this change related to?
- ➤ What happens if you don't evolve?
- ➤ What's the adaptation worth to you?

Start Close In,
David Whyte, *River Flow*

Start close in,
don't take the second step
or the third,
start with the first
thing
close in,
the step
you don't want to take.

Start with
the ground
you know,
the pale ground
beneath your feet,
your own
way to begin
the conversation.

Start with your own
question,
give up on other
people's questions,
don't let them
smother something
simple.

To hear
another's voice,
follow
your own voice,
wait until
that voice
becomes an
intimate private ear
that can
really listen
to another.

Start right now
take a small step
you can call your own
don't follow
someone else's
heroics, be humble
and focused,
start close in,
don't mistake
that other
for your own.

Untangled

Start close in,

don't take

the second step

or the third,

start with the first

thing

close in,

the step

you don't want to take.

Notes

Notes

PART 3

UNTANGLING YOUR WAY

Notes

Chapter 5:
How to Handle Your Feelings Through Change

Introduction

Throughout any time of change, you're bound to feel all kinds of feelings. It doesn't mean you can't cope. It also isn't a sign that you should give up. And, whatever the feeling, it probably won't stick around for long anyway (see my thoughts on mindfulness in Chapter 10). But, because I know how powerful those feelings can be, this chapter is here to help you when you are feeling all the emotions of change. I'll share the most common feelings you might experience and give suggestions for how you might cope with them. I've seen these come up over and over again in twenty-five years of working with people through change. You're definitely not alone.

In this chapter you'll learn how to cope when change feels:

➤ Constant

➤ Negative

➤ Fake

➤ Tricky

➤ Premature

➤ Circular

➤ Imposed

You can feel free to read the ones that apply to you now and bookmark the rest for later.

Why change doesn't feel good

Human beings are a curious mix. On the one hand, we are wired towards evolution. We need to keep changing. On the other hand, we like the status quo and are also predisposed towards homeostasis. Which means we don't like change; we gravitate towards stability. And obviously, there are times when change does feel good, when we are excited about things and looking forward with eager anticipation. We feel the flood of positive emotions and hormones in the flush of a new relationship; we get the buzz from starting to find our feet in a new job. What often isn't talked about though, is that change brings with it a whole bunch of challenging feelings, and we don't always feel we have the resources to deal with them. Whilst from a psychology and a mindfulness point of view, we are not our feelings, and they will pass, it can be helpful to have some tools to deal with them when they arise. As much as anything else, it is important to remember that you are not alone in feeling these things – every single day, thousands of people are having a similar experience as they navigate this human existence. Even today, as I write these words, I've had to remind myself that it's okay for the current changes I'm facing to feel tricky, and potentially premature. It's part of living through it. And I will get through it.

> There are times in our lives when the carousel of change just doesn't seem to stop

When change feels constant and overwhelming

There are times in our lives when the carousel of change just doesn't seem to stop. We feel like we are clinging on and it's one thing after another. And, unlike a carousel, it isn't usually fun. A dear friend of mine had a spell like that not long ago. She was working two jobs, both of which she loved, but one of which was a fixed-term appointment and relied on a business case to get it approved for the longer term. The other job was challenging and demanding. At the same time, her youngest child was heading off to university, leaving my friend and her husband empty nesters for the first time in twenty-four years. To top it all off, they got a new car for the first time in, well, forever and made the switch to electric. It was a lot of change in a short time. One of these things on its own would be enough to unnerve and unsettle us; put them all together and it just feels constant. Even the change we think we want – in this case my friend getting the new car – seems to be questionable. Not because we don't want that part of change, more because it feels like the straw that could break the camel's back. We just want to stop the change carousel and get off for a bit. We want the dizziness to stop! And that's natural – our mind longs for some place of stability, somewhere that things are not in flux. We want to have a space that we can rely on. And that's the secret to coping with these feelings.

Create some space for you. I know that sounds simple. And I also know how hard it can be. I've had to resort to putting signs on my home office door in the past to remind people in my house not to disturb me! Even the act of carving out fifteen minutes a day for yourself can feel like it takes a Herculean effort, but it is possible and, miraculously, it does make a difference! When we make a little space for ourselves, something seems to shift. It's almost as if we are giving ourselves – and others – a signal that we are serious about prioritising ourselves. Not to the exclusion of everyone and everything else, more in integration with our other responsibilities.

For my friend, this took a very practical form. She bought herself some yarn and started to knit a snuggle blanket. Every evening, she sat by the fire and spent a little time by herself, being intentional about the use of her time as well as her hands. Very soon, not only did she have a beautiful blanket to snuggle under, she also had a new perspective on the changes around her, and felt less out of control. For me, the year that I ended my relationship, moved house and was still grieving the loss of my mum, I started 'snuggle-down Sundays'. Every Sunday, I asked my daughter to take the dog out for his last walk. I'd light some candles, run a bath and slowly wind down. After my bath, I'd make us both hot chocolate with marshmallows and I'd tuck myself up in bed with the mug of soothing sweetness and a good book. Carving out that hour for myself gave me so much more in the week ahead. So today, make a little space for you. What could that look like? It doesn't have to be inside – many people find it incredibly helpful to get outside and immerse themselves in the wider world. What do you need to be able to stop the dizziness and find some inner stillness? Ask someone on your support squad to hold you accountable for what you need if that helps. Tell them you'll text them when you start your time to yourself and then again at the end. People want to help you to get out of the state of overwhelm!

When change feels negative

Sometimes we face change that just doesn't feel good. We know what we don't want, but not what we do. Once upon a time, I spent a couple of years working for a boutique consultancy. It started out with all the flush of a new romance; I felt giddy with the possibilities and potential. I could see what could result from my work there and it truly lit me up. Until one day I realised that the

CEO was never going to change; the culture was toxic, and most of the people who worked there felt trapped with no way out. I knew I needed to get out, to get back to doing my own thing and to give up on the dreams I'd had of being part of the future of that consultancy. I had to let go of the potential that they would buy out my company, but more importantly than that, I had to accept that I couldn't create the change there that I thought I could. Day by day, this realisation grew stronger, but I couldn't act on it. Something kept stopping me in my tracks. I was completely clear. I didn't want to be working there. I knew that in my core. I wanted out, to be free. I hated every minute of being in the craziness that working with the CEO involved. I can't even begin to describe the ridiculous things that happened, but they will be sadly familiar to many of you who have worked in organisations. I did not want to work for them a minute longer. But I stayed. In fact, I overstayed. Because I didn't get clear on what I actually wanted. I got so caught up in what I didn't want that, like an eclipse, it overshadowed what I did want.

You might experience this yourself in a relationship, a job, or even in the home you live in. The growing sense of restlessness and unease, and of knowing that something has to change, you just don't know what! And that's the key. When we are motivated by change that feels like a negative goal – the kind of change where we know what we *don't* want – the most powerful way to unlock change sits behind that. You need to connect with what you *do* want instead. What's the thing that you really want to have? Write that down. You might want to link back to the work in Chapter 4 on finding your bigger picture. What matters to you? You might know you don't want to be in a relationship with someone anymore – what do you want instead? You might not want to be working the long hours you're working right now – what's your dream? It might be that you are totally fed up with your current job or way of living – paint the picture of what you do desire. Only when the vision of the future becomes more compelling than the current reality will you find the courage to make the change. The absence of something is not enough to pull you forward. You have to find the thing you want. And then start making it real. For me,

> Only when the vision of the future becomes more compelling than the current reality will you find the courage to make the change

I wanted the freedom to be able to do the work I wanted in a way that felt right. I longed to be working with people who respected me, and I wanted to have strong trust-based relationships. I left. Eventually. And it felt so liberating.

When change feels false or fake

Sometimes we get part-way through creating a change in our lives and then, one day, we wake up and think, *what am I doing?* You might have been working at it for months, or even years. You've poured your heart and soul into it and then the alarm goes off one morning, and before your feet even hit the floor, the realisation hits you between the eyes. You don't want this. It's not what you're after. This often happens with people before I start to work with them. They get stuck into change that they think they want, without confirming that the goal is real.

I actually think there are few feelings that hit harder in change than the feeling that you've been pursuing a fake dream. It's not that you are a fake. Or even that you set out to follow this thing believing anything other than that it was a genuine ambition or hope. But it can happen along the way, that you realise you've been chasing rainbows. So how does it happen? I blame it on the Instagram effect (other social media channels are available and cause similar false goals). We see something online, or in someone else's life, and we become convinced that we want it. At a simple level that might be something small (I'm currently longing for some new stationery I've got my eye on). At a different level, we end up craving a lifestyle or way of being. We become certain that we want to have a new job, or take a new course, or change up our house for the eleventh time this year. It's something psychologists call the primacy and recency effect. We remember what we saw last. So, when we immerse ourselves in the online world, we can become hooked on the ideal, or rather, on someone else's version of ideal. When you recognise that change doesn't feel like it's totally in line with what truly matters to you, it can be a useful time to reconnect with your values or to journal and keep asking yourself what you want. For the next week, try to note down at least five answers to the question 'what do you want?', and see what patterns emerge. If you want to have a living room sanctuary or to train as a yoga teacher, it will show up in your answers.

I'll finish with a word of caution. Sometimes change that feels fake is a form of zigzag or circular change, which I'll come to soon. You might be heading in the right overall direction, but you're slightly off the most direct route. It can be helpful to make time to listen to yourself, without undue outside influence. What do you want? What if nobody ever knew – would you still want to run the marathon? Are you doing it for yourself? Or are you doing it to try to gain approval from people whose opinions don't even matter? Revisit the section on 'What do you want?' in Chapter 4 if you need more clarity on what you long for.

When change feels impossible

There are times when change feels impossible. When you feel trapped, stuck and completely without options. Or, if there are options, they seem impossible to achieve, wildly out of reach, or simply too terrifying to comprehend. Reading this now, you may be in the thick of such times. I want you to know that you are not alone. You are never alone. When you sit in the heat of the impossibility of change, you sit with others who are facing the same. The feelings you are experiencing can feel isolating, they are in fact a core part of humanity. You are not the first to feel like this and you won't be the last. And, while it may feel completely incomprehensible to you right now, you will get through this. You will live through this change. You will come through the other side. Like walking on fire, you are capable of more than you can ever imagine. I know this because I have been there too, facing the impossible. And I came through the other side. As will you.

I had avoided facing my financial situation for months. Many months. I sat cross-legged on the floor, heart racing, palms sweating. I knew it was time. Stacked in front of me were piles of paper. Envelopes mostly. Brown. Unopened. Metallic tastes filled my mouth. Was I actually going to vomit? *No, breathe. It's time. Baby steps. Just start with one.* Cautiously, as if reaching for something with fangs, I picked up the first envelope. Sealed. Contents unknown but feared. Thoughts raced through my mind: *Am I going to prison? Is this the end? Regardless, I know I am a failure.* Closing my eyes, I took another deep breath. *I can do this. I can do this.* I picked at the edge of the seal and slid my finger along the length of the envelope. Nothing bit me. It was, after all, just a letter. A final demand. A threat. But also, just a letter. I took a sharp breath in. *Keep breathing,* I told myself. *I can do this. I can do this.* I separated the contents and the envelope. And I reached for the next one in the pile...

Building for months, this was the day when I finally started to face the problem. I had eventually reached the stage where the fear of

> Glaciers create huge change. It's not done at pace. Start slow and trust yourself

inaction was greater than the fear of taking action. I recognised that the only way I was going to create change was to actually stare into the abyss and start with what was in front of me. Many, many months of hard work followed, until years later I reached the point where I could finally say that I was debt free (other than my mortgage) and I always will be. I will never owe anyone money again. For me, it's not worth it. I can now stand, clean and clear, and know that nobody can ever chase me for money again. The first steps though, sitting on that floor, were without doubt the hardest. The day when I said to myself, *'okay, enough, today we take action, and face that fear'*.

And that's where you start too. With the first steps. The thing that's closest to you. As the poet David Whyte says in *Start Close In*, 'the step you don't want to take'. Break the change down into the smallest steps possible, and start with the first one. Crawl, if you have to. Take it slower than a slow thing on a slow day. But start. Glaciers create huge change. It's not done at pace. Start slow and trust yourself. You can do this.

When change feels premature

This is what I think of as the challenge of false starts. Sometimes we get ahead of ourselves. We can take off head first into change and then realise we weren't ready. Oops! This is different from the fake change above – it's more a case of too much, too soon. A bit like when marathon runners start out strong, only to struggle halfway.

Not that I'm a marathon runner, but I've sometimes worked with clients who head off into creating change and, before they know it, they realise it's been a false start. It's easy to do, particularly if you tend to get excited about new ideas or thoughts, or if you are truly fed up with the current state of affairs. Obviously, this relates much more to change we choose than change that gets thrown in our path. However, it can also happen with reactive change. We think we know what's happened, but it's actually only the start of a bigger change. A bit like if you tug at a ball of string and then keep pulling at it.

Many years ago, I designed and built a house with my (now ex-) husband. We worked with a designer and had a blueprint almost complete. Then the relationship with the designer deteriorated, and he started to become a man who just kept saying 'no'. It didn't feel like we were going to get the house we wanted, so we ended our contract with him. I went looking for an architect to finish the design and help us to get planning permission. We thought we knew our aim: someone to finish the drawings and get us to the point where we could start to build. Until we met Jenny Jones. Jenny was an architect with a commercial background. She'd never designed a house. I met her one evening at the plot of land we'd bought, both of us in wellies, her smile larger than life. Roaming over the land and explaining why I loved it, she took me back to what had captivated me in the first place. She reminded me that I wanted to have the house be connected with the land, to have free flow into the garden. She highlighted the need for privacy and the potential to expand the house over time. She connected me with my bigger dream. And she firmly and clearly told me that she didn't think the design we had worked on so far would give us what we wanted. We'd made a massive false start. Luckily, we hadn't gone too far, although it seemed a big decision to stop what we were doing at the time. But we stopped. We put the original design aside and I asked Jenny to design the house she could see in her mind's eye. The house we eventually built. Having the courage to recognise a false start and to stop the path you're on is hard. And it's worth it. We ended up with the dream house – at least until our marriage ended. If we'd kept going with the initial design, we would have had a nice house in a great location, but we would never have achieved the dream.

The way I'm going to suggest you handle this is going to sound counter-intuitive. It's to forbid yourself to make any further changes for a set amount of time. Ban yourself. Let's imagine you've started off down the road of creating changes in your home or even looking for a new one. Things start to happen; you maybe even make an offer on a new property and then it comes unstuck for some reason. Pause. Literally stop. No changes to your current property. No moves on any new potential homes. Freeze for a set amount of time. Maybe a month. Maybe longer. You might be asking what you do during the pause. Take the time to reflect. That might mean talking to a friend about what matters. Or you might want to write answers in your journal to some prompt questions from the section in Chapter 4 on what's important about the change. What happens when you do this is that you realise what you actually want. Maybe within a month you go a little bit crazy and discover that you absolutely have to move. You might notice that, actually, you were just bored, and you've found another way to fill that need. Or perhaps you recognise that you want to channel your creativity into your home because it's a bigger season of change. When we freeze, we leave space for the real change to show itself. And similarly, if the change is being thrown at you, you leave space for the true nature of that change to show itself. From there you can step more fully into living with it and through it. So, notice when change feels premature and pause.

When change feels circular or zigzag

Sometimes it feels like change follows anything but a straight line. We zigzag around, occasionally even feeling like we are going round in circles. It can seem like the destination, wherever that may be, is out of reach. This can feel beyond frustrating, particularly if we have clarity about what we want and why it's important to us. In my teens when I was windsurfing, the thing that always confused me the most is that you don't go in a straight line from where you are to where you want to be. I'm not sure I ever fully understood why, but you have to 'tack' which, in windsurfing and sailing terms, means you go in a zigzag. It's got something to do with the wind and wanting to make the most of it. The sail needs to be at an angle in relation to the direction of the wind. It actually is the quickest and most efficient way to get from your starting point to your destination. And sometimes the same is true for change. We start at point *a* and we want to go to point *b*, but the quickest and most effective way to get there isn't to go as the bird flies, it's to go in a zigzag. For change, this might look like unexpected bumps in the road. Maybe you're looking for a new job; you're clear on what you want, and you head off towards it. But along the way you end up having a conversation with someone who connects you with somebody else. Before you know it, you're considering retraining for a different career or even relocating to a different country. Sometimes the diversions are smaller, but the change still feels zigzag or even circular. You might get a sense that you've been here before as you fill out the umpteenth application form.

I do believe this sense of circular change can bring us benefits.

That we might stumble across some magic along the way, that takes us into a different, more fulfilling type of change. And it can sometimes be hard to recognise that, when we're in the thick of it. Here's an activity you can use to help you stay connected to your own change priorities, while remaining open to new things that might appear. I used to use this exercise with my daughter when she was younger and wanted to keep all her story books forever. Basically, you're choosing one thing over another, repeatedly, to see what bubbles up as the most important. For us, it was a way to make sure she didn't actually need her own library by the age of twelve. For you, it can help you to identify what aspect of change you're facing that's the most important.

Priority-sifting

You'll need paper and pen for this; sticky notes will do – the pieces of paper don't have to be big. On each piece of paper, you're going to write one aspect of the current change that's facing you. Each piece of paper is something that's a priority for you. Think about what matters to you from Chapter 1 and get more specific for this actual change you're looking at. What matters to you most? Let's stick with job or career change as an example. You might write the following, each one on a different piece of paper:

- I want to use my core skills.
- I want to have fun.
- I want to work with people I respect.
- I want to get paid well.
- I want to be able to work flexibly.
- I want to make a difference.

Maybe you know these things, and then you have a conversation with someone, and they offer you a job that's three hundred miles away. Suddenly, you realise you have another thing to write down:

➡ I want to work close to home.

So now we can use the pieces of paper to prioritise. Pick up two of the pieces of paper, and decide which one is more important to you. Set the other one aside, but don't get rid of it. It's still important to you. Now pick up a third piece of paper and compare it to the first one. Which one is more important to you from those two? Again, set the other one aside. Repeat this process until you know which is your top priority for this change, for now. Write it down in your journal or here and use it as a guide. Make a note of the other things that you wrote down because they also matter.

Holding onto your priorities and your ultimate destination will guide you through the zig and the zag. It gives you something to navigate by.

When change feels imposed

There are times when change feels imposed. And there are also times when it is imposed. And in both of these, we can often feel powerless and helpless, buffeted on the ocean of our own lives. Change that feels like it comes from outside us can feel threatening, because it feels like we aren't in control, and most of us don't like that feeling. Even people who do things like jumping out of planes are actually in control because they are choosing what control they release or hand over to someone else.

When I lost my job at the start of the 2009 recession, I felt completely out of control. It seemed like everything I had known was pulled from under my feet. I didn't know what on earth to do next. It's partly why I told my husband to put champagne in the fridge when I found out I didn't have a job. I needed to have control. I wanted to feel less cast out to sea. So, I chose to control the tiniest of things. I also believe this is why it's important for us to give children a sense of control. Even if it's a choice between two things – do you want to wear this jacket or that coat? As human beings, we need to feel we have a sense of agency. We need to be able to choose.

Stephen Covey identified that there are things that concern us and then there are things that we can influence. His son took this further to say that there are things that we can control. This can be a helpful way to make a map of things when we feel powerless. Draw three circles, one inside the other, like a target. The innermost circle is the things you can control; the middle circle is the things you can influence; and the outermost circle is things that concern you. You can then write things into each circle. Your aim is to increase the things in the inner two circles (the things you can control and influence) and reduce the things in the outer circle (that concern you). So even in change that comes our way, such as job loss or bereavement, there are clearly things that belong in the outer circle, including the event itself, how other people react, what it means in terms of immediate practicalities. But we can broaden the inner circles. We can take more control over how we react. We can make choices about what we do with our time. We can choose how we remember a loved one, and what we do to start looking for a new job. Expanding your circles of control and influence will help you to both *feel* less out of control and actually *be* less out of control. There are times to go with the wind and see what happens, and, when change feels overwhelming and deeply uncertain, it can be helpful to temporarily take steps to feel more in control.

Summary

When Change Feels...	Try This...
Constant	Make space for yourself
	Revisit self-care
Negative	Paint the picture of what you do want
	Revisit your bigger picture
Fake	Reconnect with your values
	Journal on what you really want
Impossible	Start close in with the step you don't want to take
	Go slower than a slow thing
Premature	Pause
	Forbid yourself to change
Circular or zigzag	Prioritise your destination
	Stay open to the magic
Imposed	Identify what you can control
	Identify what you can influence

Chapter 6:
How to Ride the Waves of Change

Introduction

In living through change, there are going to be times when we fail, and there will also be times when we succeed. And there will be times when we aren't quite sure which of those is happening. In one sense, it doesn't really matter. What matters most is making our way through life, learning as we go and honouring our values and purpose. But most of us are trained from a young age to make critical assessments of what's good and what's bad. Remember the story of the farmer from Chapter 4? We may not actually know what's good and what's bad, but we try to work it out. It's all part of life's cycles. What happens today informs and influences what happens tomorrow. What seems like a disaster today may actually turn out to be the biggest gift of all. When I lost my job at the end of 2008, a friend and colleague gave me a card. On the inside she'd written that this could turn out to be the best thing that happened to me. I was actually a bit hurt when I opened it. Didn't she get it at all? At the time, staring into a future with no income and a husband and child depending on me, I thought she was crazy. I had lost my job. I didn't even know who I was anymore. I was angry with the situation, and I felt hopeless about my future. How on earth could this be the best thing that had ever happened to me?! But, in the end, she was right. Losing my job became the catalyst to me retraining, following my absolute passion, building a business that I love, and ultimately writing this book. Maybe she wasn't so crazy after all!

In this chapter I'm going to share with you the reasons we find it so hard to let go and release ourselves from our current lives or patterns. I'll show you how to do so. We will also look at your relationship with failure, because it's so closely related. We'll finish this section by looking at success and how we can celebrate. That's where we'll also look at what you want to take forward with you into the next phase of your life. These chapters are closely linked. If you've got the time to immerse yourself in them together, I would do that. You'll start to see how success and failure are intricately linked and how, in living with change, we need to get more comfortable with both. By the end of this chapter you will:

- Understand what makes it difficult to let go
- Have identified what no longer serves you
- Know how to let go of the old
- Recognise where you are failing
- Realise that failing at something does not make you a failure
- Know how to pick yourself back up when you fall
- Understand how to learn from your failures

Why letting go is hard

Maria had been married to her charming, slightly off-beat husband for over ten years. In the beginning, he'd felt like a great match, but lately she wasn't so sure. Despite their having kids together, increasingly she wondered if they might be better off apart. In each of her coaching sessions, her emotions were just below the surface. She'd bite her lip. Her hands fidgeted. The sparkle of tears that couldn't yet fall was almost always visible. She came to me to help her work through how she was feeling and to look at what she could do to move forward with her life. As our work together evolved, she became increasingly desperate with the need to change her situation. Living in the same house as her husband, she felt constantly compromised, she felt like she couldn't actually live the way she wanted to. She needed to change. In reality, she realised she needed to let go: of her husband, of their marriage and of the life she had dreamed they would have together. But it took her months. The weeks went by, and she stayed. Each time we had a coaching session, something would have come up that got in the way. Despite all the clarity she had, she just couldn't let go. What made it so hard? What stopped her? Like a wobbly tooth that just won't come out when you're a kid, she clung on week after week after week.

From years of working with coaching clients, facing professional and personal change, I can categorically say we do not find it easy to let go. We cling on. As human beings, we are wired to have hope. To stay with situations, people, jobs that don't serve us, in the belief that things will get better. Or sometimes in the pursuit of complete certainty, a guarantee that it

> Like a wobbly tooth that just won't come out when you're a kid, she clung on

will work out. And we can never have complete certainty. We will always have doubts. We will always be unsure. Because we never know what the future will bring, we can never guarantee that we are making a move for the better. We have to take it on good faith. We have to trust ourselves and believe that we are making the best decision that we can, with what we have and what we know in this moment. We have to be what I call 'certain enough'. And ultimately, we then need to move forward from there. As my client ultimately did. She stepped out into the future. Uncertain, but certain enough, she started to let go of what no longer served her. Gradually, with each step that she took, she grew in her belief, and she grew in her confidence that she was making the right decision. She created a new life for herself and her children and she has never looked back.

How to identify what no longer serves you

The first step in letting go is, of course, to recognise what's not working for you. And in some cases that might be something you can change, while in other cases you might need to let go. Let's stay with my client who recognised that her marriage was no longer serving her. What she noticed to begin with was her feelings. She felt frustrated with her husband; she was irritated by his behaviours; and she became insecure in their relationship. Noticing your feelings is the starting point for identifying what's not working. Feelings of frustration, irritation, despondence and, ultimately, withdrawal can be warning signs that something needs to change. As I said before, it's perfectly possible to create changes within your existing situation. I'm not for a minute saying that everyone who feels frustrated in their job needs to resign, or that every single person who feels irritated by their partner needs to end the relationship! I'm suggesting that it is a sign that something isn't working, and it offers an opportunity to change things – the starting point is usually to begin where you are, to try and find a way to have less frustration at work and to have a more harmonious relationship with a partner.

Here's a short activity to help you notice some of the things that might not quite be working for you right now. You can simply write endings to these sentences with whatever springs to mind. If you've done the wheel of life activity in Chapter 4 under 'What's the ideal?', you might use the themes from the wheel of life as starting points and complete the sentences for all or some of the slices in the wheel, e.g. relationship, health and fitness, community. The aim is to keep writing until you start to unearth what isn't actually working for you anymore. Sometimes that comes quickly and sometimes we need to dig a bit deeper. Let's look at an example to help you get started. If I am frustrated in my job, I might write things like 'I can't cope with the unreasonable short deadlines. I can't cope with my boss making unfair demands. I can't cope with always feeling like I'm letting my kids down. I can't cope with feeling like I'm always on the back foot. I can't cope with never having space or time to think. I can't cope with always feeling like I'm having to catch up' etc. When you step back and look at what you've written, you might realise that it's not actually the job that needs to change; it might be that you need to take some time out each week to plan and be proactive. Start by writing whatever comes to mind for these sentences:

- ➡ I can't cope with...
- ➡ I get frustrated with...
- ➡ It would drive me crazy if... lasted forever
- ➡ I feel compromised when...
- ➡ I'm ready to change...
- ➡ I want more...
- ➡ I want less...

Write as many things as you can for each sentence, and then have a look to see what themes emerge. You might notice that there are specific things that are irritating you, or your answers might point to a particular aspect in your life that you are ready to change. If you find it hard to spot the themes, you can either ask a friend to help you, or write each one on a sticky note and move them around on a table until you can see which ones belong together.

I also used to believe that letting go of things was failure. In fact, I don't think I'll ever forget the first time that I decided to *not* keep going with something. I was working on an award in Guiding (Girl Scouts in North America). I was in my mid-teens and had achieved all the badges and awards and certificates I'd ever attempted. I was, in slightly geeky teenage ways, successful. It wasn't in my nature or in my upbringing to give up. If you set your mind on something, you kept going until you'd finished it. You didn't bail – that was a sign of weakness, a failing. So, when I was around sixteen years old, it genuinely took courage for me to say, 'No. I'm going to stop now. I'm not going to finish this award.' It was a huge deal. Massive. I'd been working on this thing for months. The expectation was that I'd get it done. It was the Queen's Guide award, the greatest achievement for Guiding in the UK. Everyone expected me to finish it. But I didn't want it enough for the sacrifices it involved. I wasn't hungry enough to put other things on hold or to make the time to prioritise it. It wasn't the right choice for me. I chose to let go. That was the right choice for me. And it was the very opposite of failing. I was successful at choosing what mattered to me.

How to let go of the old

Now that you've identified what might not be serving you anymore, it's time to actually let go of it. As I said before, letting go might mean making changes exactly where you are. You might want to release your expectations about a job that you're in, or release the way you've previously communicated with your children or other family members.

It can be helpful to find some physically symbolic way of letting go of the old. You might notice that part of you actually still wants to hold on and is finding it hard to release what's no longer serving you. Somehow when we come to the physical act of release, we have to confront any residual hanging on. Many years ago, we worked with a leadership team who had come together as the result of a merger of two organisations. We were running a residential workshop with them to help them come together for the new company. We had chosen a theme of ships and sailing, though I can't remember why. We had told them they could bring three things from the old organisation with them on to the new, metaphorical ship. We were honouring that there were things from the legacy organisation that they would want to keep, such as ways of working, client focus or how they collaborated. We then invited them to make paper boats, to release the legacy of their previous organisation, and we asked them to write what they were letting go of on the paper boats before sailing them off down a stream in the grounds of the hotel. Each leader in turn floated their boat on the water, releasing what was no longer needed, in readiness for the new future organisation. In a highly poignant moment, as we left the stream to head back into the meeting room, I noticed that one boat was still sitting on the tiny bridge that crossed the river. Created by the team member who was most resistant to change, this boat never made it into the water. In a small but powerful gesture, this leader had indicated that they were not yet ready to let go. We worked with that individual in one-to-one coaching for many months following that day, but I still remember the image of that boat, propped up against a stone wall. Be kind to yourself if you find it hard to release and let go. It's not easy, but you will do so when the time is right.

Here are five ways you could use to let go of the old:

> Be kind to yourself if you find it hard to release and let go

You can write the things that you want to let go of on pieces of paper and burn them in a fire. Many people do this at the end of the year, to release what they don't want to take with them into the next year. As you burn each piece of paper, you can say out loud what you are choosing to release. You can also get wish paper, which burns in a mesmerising way and almost lets the words float up into the air.

- ➤ You can write the words on paper and bury what no longer serves you.

- ➤ You can write the words on pebbles (in eco-friendly pen or pencil) and throw them into a lake or pond. The sound of the splash of letting go can be therapeutic.

- ➤ You can even write what you're releasing on pieces of toilet paper and flush them down the toilet! What a way to get rid of crap that's no longer serving you!

- ➤ One other way to let go, if you live near the sea, is to write the words in the sand and let the waves take them away.

Please remember that you get to do this your way. The suggestions above are meant to help you think through what you'd like to do, and I'd love you to come up with your own ideas. I've let go of things in so many different ways in the past. Sometimes I've even combined them into a small ritual-type ceremony. For example, when I had done a significant piece of healing to do with stories from long ago, I got a photo of myself from that age and I wrote a letter to someone else who had been involved. I released the pain and hurt and said what I needed to say. I went to a significant place relating to what happened, and I buried the letter and the photograph. Then I planted a small plant in the same site, so that something good could grow from the painful experience.

I also tend to do something to let go of things at the end of each year. Usually it involves fire and burning what I don't want to take into the new year. I'll write down the words for what I'm leaving behind, and then burn them. It's liberating and helps to release what I don't need in my life anymore. What's going to help you feel more free? It's time to do it your way!

How to handle it when it doesn't work out like you hoped

Sometimes things don't go according to plan. You do not need me to tell you that. Life throws us curveballs; the proverbial hits the fan. We sit down and think, *hang on, that was not supposed to happen like that*. We wake up and realise that we've been climbing the ladder, only to notice it was propped up against a different wall than we thought it was. In living through change, we are signing up for the unknown. We can never predict what will happen, and sometimes the biggest, boldest, most beautiful hopes we have for our future end up smashed on the rocks. Here are some steps to take when things don't go the way you thought they would:

Step 1: Pause

It can be tempting to simply keep going. I've done that; it's never a good idea. Like the day when I fell off a chair in the middle of delivering a training session and barely even paused for breath. We want to keep going, somehow convinced that we can style it out. That if we keep going, we don't need to acknowledge the disappointment, hurt or upset. And we need to pause. It matters that we take time and space before we get stuck into the next thing. We need to honour our experience, even when it sucks. When we do that, we give ourselves the potential to change what happens next. We put ourselves back in the driving seat.

Step 2: Look at what has worked

Believe me, I'm the best at beating myself up and, when things don't go the way I envisaged, I can focus on what went wrong. And there is a time and a place for that. But it's equally important to take the time to understand what did work. It can be so easy to think that nothing did, that the whole thing was a disaster. In reality, that's rarely the case. When I've lost out on big pieces of work, I do have to force myself to look at what we did well. When we can recognise what's worked, we can build on it. If we focus only on the negative, we deprive ourselves of that gift.

Step 3: Reconnect with what matters

Remember all that work we did to understand why this change is important to you? It's time to dig it out, flick back to those pages in your journal and remind yourself what truly matters. Maybe this version didn't work out. That's giving you information. And the chances are you've just realised how important the thing is to you. When things didn't work out in my relationship, I took the time to heal. I was then able to revisit what mattered and recognise that I do thrive with connection. In reality, that can come from a partner, but it can also come from friends, family and even work colleagues. And that leads to step 4.

Step 4: Redesign what needs to be different

Once you've reconnected with what matters, you can look at how you can live it differently. For me, when I realised that it truly is important to me to have connection in my life, I started to become much more intentional about spending time with family and friends, even when I didn't want to. I also made sure that I put time in my diary every week to connect with former clients and colleagues. It wasn't the same as starting a new relationship, but it was important to me as a way of actually living with connection in my life.

Step 5: Start again

When things don't work out, eventually you'll dust yourself off and start again. You'll decide to train for another marathon after an injury stops you from completing the one you've trained for. You'll start dating after getting divorced. You'll put yourself up for promotion at work after being passed over the time before. You are a daring, courageous human being. It may take time. It will take bravery. And I know you can do it.

The more I'm brave and put myself into new and challenging situations, the higher the risk that it's not going to work out the way I want it to. I can choose to play safe, and then there's less risk. As a friend of mine said recently, 'It's amazing how many things don't go wrong when I'm sitting on my sofa.' The thing is, I'm not someone to live my life sitting on a sofa, so when I make moves, there will be times when it doesn't work out. Many years ago, I had a stark reminder of this. It was probably the biggest time when, publicly, things didn't go the way I wanted them to. I'm sharing it here because we all have times when the dream does not become the reality, and I want to remind you that you will get through it, dust yourself down and get back up again with new insight and awareness.

Dark surroundings, people dressed in their finery. The largest formal dinner in Scotland in over three hundred years. Two thousand business leaders gathered to recognise excellence in Scottish business. The atmosphere was electric, a heady mix of anticipation, celebration and entertainment. Candles lit the finest of menus. Comedian Michael McIntyre compered the evening, lighting up the stage in his inimitable style.

Sir Richard Branson gave the keynote address, dressed, as only he could be, in a denim tuxedo created by Levi's. His words connected deeply with my ethos on business. He talked passionately about the ways in which business can, and should be, a force for good. As he spoke, my hopes grew. Perhaps we could be in with a chance to win the new business of the year award? His views and mine aligned. I started Firefly with a mission. I believed in the power of collaboration. The guests I'd invited were those who I thought would benefit most from being there, not those I wanted to impress.

We were shortlisted, and it had felt like an outside chance that we'd win. I'd entered more to get feedback, to raise awareness of the business and also to be able to attend and host a table for my guests. But as he spoke, my excitement grew. My guests at our table enjoyed their dinner. I barely ate a crumb. It was the most expensive meal I've ever paid for, and I didn't eat any of it. Thoughts of *what if* raced through my head. If we won, what would be different? If we won, what would that say about Firefly as a business? If we didn't win, what might change? It felt like everything and nothing rested on those words that night. I was dressed in anticipation of having to walk on to the stage to collect an award, but I had no idea if that was really likely or even possible. The adrenaline raced through my veins, waves of nausea and an ever-changing tide of 'maybe we have, maybe we haven't' washed over me.

Against a background murmuring of polite business chat, they announced the category of new business of the year. Highlighted on the huge screens behind Sir Richard were the names of three new businesses in the shortlist. It hardly seemed possible that Firefly was on the screen – the dream that I'd had for a business was already being recognised in that environment. The idea and the vision had become real, and now, here it was in front of two thousand people. It felt incredible, and I also felt sick as the words 'and the winner of the new business of the year 2014 is...' came out of Sir Richard's mouth. Breathless, I waited, tipped over the edge, as he finished the sentence, '...Hunter Adams'. My heart plummeted as my hands automatically started to applaud, and my face formed its way into a celebratory smile. I was completely gutted. But now was not the time for that. Tears could flow later. Surrounded by my team, select clients and invited guests, I rallied myself. 'It was amazing to get shortlisted. Hunter Adams is a great business. Let's make sure we have a great night.' And inside I fell apart a little. But I don't regret submitting our application. I don't regret giving it all that I had. And I don't regret aiming high. I had to give it everything. And I learned a lot in the process. That night was one of my biggest lessons in not being able to control the outcome, but it was also one of the biggest reminders that if you reach for the moon, you will land among the stars. That night was one to hold in my memories forever. Plus, I still have the dress, and the shoes.

Why failing at something does not make you a failure

A quick Google search for quotes on failure will show you how intricately success and failure are linked. Thomas Edison famously once said that he had not failed to make a light bulb, he had succeeded at finding another way *not* to make one.

When we face change, we will encounter failures and setbacks. What is absolutely vital is that we don't translate those failings into believing that we *are* failures. Separating the thing that has happened from who we are as human beings is what makes it possible to keep going. If something happens and I believe that I *have* failed at it, I'm going to pick myself up, dust myself down and try again. If something happens and I believe that I *am* a failure, I'm much more likely to give up, hide under the nearest rock and not come back out again, or at least not want to. But the distinction is sometimes easier to say and think, than it is to feel and believe. The reality is that we can often get caught up believing that our very being is defined by our results.

In entrepreneurship, the most successful business creators know that they will fail. The trick they learn early on is to fail fast and fail forward. Lisa Nichols describes it like this 'Abundant thinkers look for the lesson in any situation where they didn't get the outcome they wanted. They fail, but they also move forward with greater clarity and better answers on how to maximise the next great idea' (*Abundance Now*). What that means is that they realise the most helpful type of failure is one that brings them momentum, when they can take what they've learned from what's happened, and use it to improve. Let's look at what that means in a change context.

For change you choose, you're going to have times where it just doesn't work or come together. Let's imagine you want to find a new job or get a promotion at work. Chances are, you won't be successful with your first application. As much as you might do all the preparation, and get yourself set up for the job offer, it just might not happen first time around. You might get feedback that there were other candidates who were more qualified than you. It's conceivable that you could say something stupid in the interview (we can all make mistakes when we're feeling under pressure). You can also just sometimes not be a good fit for a role or even an organisation.

I once had an interview for a job many years ago, where the recruitment consultant was in the room when I met with the chief executive for my interview. I was excited about the job and had tons of questions. I could totally see myself in the role and wanted to learn more about the priorities and the way things worked in the organisation. I felt we had a good conversation, but I didn't get the job, and I was actually genuinely surprised. The biggest feedback I got from the recruitment consultant was that I asked too many questions! Looking back, I had probably put myself too far into the position of imagining I had been successful and secured the post. I guess it didn't come across too well. Potentially it could have looked like I was dominating the interview, which wasn't my intention at all. I had failed. The very definition of failure. I went for an interview, and I didn't get the job. I wanted to crawl under a rock and never come out. I felt defeated, not good enough and like I never, ever wanted to go

> When we are already feeling raw from dealing with reactive change, any sense of failure can hit us even harder

for another job again. I felt like a failure. But I was not a failure. I had in fact learned from the experience and would go on to bigger and brighter things in the future. Not only did the feedback help me, but it's also helped my clients, particularly those looking for new jobs. The way I set them up for interviews is informed by my own experience. I failed, but it didn't make me a failure.

Before we look at how to get yourself back up again, I want to add in some thoughts about what happens when the failure arises when you're facing change that life throws at you. When we are already feeling raw from dealing with reactive change, any sense of failure can hit us even harder. When I was already struggling with grief from losing my mum and my relationship ending, anything that didn't work out took on a greater significance. It's one of the reasons why self-compassion and self-care matter so much when we're going through change we didn't choose. At times it makes me want to scream. Not only am I dealing with some of the biggest stuff that life throws at me, but now I need to take care of myself as well?! That just seems like the ultimate kicker. When all I wanted to do was hide and not face the world after Mum died, there were days when I did just stay under the bedcovers. A day or two of that is okay; in fact, sometimes it is exactly what you need. And then there comes a point where you have to treat yourself like you would treat a dear friend. Nudge yourself to take some action. Put the chocolate away. Take a shower. Do what you need to, to get yourself back up again. Put the failure into perspective – it's part of the picture, not the whole picture. And, vitally, it does not define who you are. You are not a failure, even when you fail spectacularly.

- What does failure mean to you?
- What would your life be like if you'd never failed?
- What's a helpful belief for you to hold about failure?

How to pick yourself back up

You've hit the deck, fallen flat on your face and failed spectacularly (or even just a little bit). Whatever you were trying to do, it hasn't worked. Remember that this does not make you a failure, so how on earth do you get back up again? Because the old saying, that it doesn't matter how many times you fall over as long as you get up more, applies here. I haven't always had strong muscles for getting back up. I've had to develop them. When I first tried to learn snowboarding, I fell over so many times I thought my body would never forgive me. Each time I'd get back up again and try over. It was fun. At least the first few times. Throughout the course of that first day on the slopes, my body got more and more tired. Eventually I was exhausted. Lying on my back on the snow, in the middle of the afternoon, I didn't think I actually had it in me to get back up. I was laughing, but only from slight hysteria and an edge of fear and failure – what if I actually couldn't do this? I joked with my sister that they must sweep the slopes at the end of the day, and they'd sweep me down the hill then. Did I have it in me to get back up? Yes. Ultimately, I somehow dug deep, found what little physical energy I had left and pulled myself over on to my side and back up to standing. I was done for the day, but I had picked myself back up for a fresh start in the morning.

When Brené Brown wrote *Daring Greatly*, she says she always knew she would have to write the subsequent volume *Rising Strong*, because her research showed that if we are brave and daring, we will fall and we will fail. She recognised that she would need to teach people how to get back up. It's actually the fourth skill set of daring leadership. The ability to get back up again after a knock-back or setback determines what happens next, not the act of falling. There are three stages for getting back up again that she outlines in *Rising Strong*, and if you find yourself falling regularly, I'd suggest you read the full book.

Stage 1 is when we recognise that we've fallen flat on our face, and we start to get curious about our feelings. The aim is to understand how what we're feeling relates to our thoughts and actions. In this way, it's similar to cognitive behavioural therapy, which helps us to look at how our thoughts, feelings, physical sensations and behaviours are related to each other, so that we can create changes in our own patterns.

Stage 2 is when we then get curious about the stories that we're making up. Human beings are incredible at making up stories and, once we do so, we tend to act as if they are real. This step is about breaking that connection and pausing long enough to notice what we're making up. We start to notice patterns. From there, we can start to notice what might need to change if we are to move forward from here in a different way.

Stage 3 is when we move that insight from our heads into our hearts and change how we act by writing a new story. We write a new future for ourselves. Similar to the 'application' stage of the experiential learning cycle that I share in the next section, where we look at learning from failure, this is where the new insight gets converted into new action.

Don't even try to learn from your failures straight away

The next time you fall and don't know how to get back up, try these steps and see what you notice. What's different for you this time? You'll probably find it easier to get back up and to do so quicker. And that means you're ready for your next change – whenever and wherever that arises.

How to learn from your failures

Don't even try to learn from your failures straight away. Read that again – it's important. When you fail, and you get yourself back up again, you can't learn the lessons straight away; give yourself time. Firstly, you might need to nurse your ego. You might be feeling a bit silly. Perhaps you're judging yourself for even trying to do something different in the first place. We've all had times when we start with the recriminations and self-criticism. You know the script: 'how could you have been so stupid?', 'what were you thinking?', 'you've done it again, you always...'. When your head is in that space, you don't stand a chance at identifying what you can learn from this. The only thing you'll identify is not to do the thing again, whatever it was.

Secondly, you will find the learning becomes a lot clearer after you allow things to settle. It's like trying to make sense of a close-up picture. You know those quiz questions where they show you a zoomed-in image of something like a plug or a hairbrush bristle, and you have to work out what it is? If you try to identify, and then apply the lessons straight away, you're just too close. You won't see what needs to be learned from the situation.

When I was lying on my back in the snow, giggling and trying to summon the energy to get back up again, it was pointless for me to think about how to become better at snowboarding. I didn't have the brain power, let alone the muscle strength, to work anything out. I needed to get myself to stand up again. It was important that I didn't just actually lie there all night and turn into an ice sculpture. But it was not the time to start to learn from it. I needed to rest, get some sleep, ease my body, and then I could work out how to stay upright more of the time in subsequent days. It takes perspective to be able to step back, reflect on what happened and what you could do differently, or how you could handle things differently in the future. Be kind to yourself and don't expect to jump straight to the learnings.

Once some time has passed and you are able to look at what's happened with a dose of self-compassion and maybe even a little humour, you can start to process the learning. There's a simple structure we use in experiential learning to help people debrief their experience. Write yourself notes on the following:

What did you experience?

Here you want to focus on writing the specifics of what happened, without any interpretation or analysis. Let's take that example of the job I didn't get when I asked lots of questions in the interview. Here's what I experienced: I applied for a job. I was excited about the role. I was very outgoing in the interview. I asked lots of questions. We had a full conversation. (Notice that I'm sticking with what happened, the facts of the situation.)

What did you learn (or relearn, because sometimes life keeps handing us the same lessons on a silver platter!)?

Here you are looking to identify what you learned as specifically as you can. Returning to my example, here are some things I might capture from this situation: I learned that I can get enthusiastic and it can sometimes overtake me; I learned that it's important to have balance in an interview; I learned that it could be helpful to identify my top two or three questions before the interview; I learned that I can get helpful feedback from the recruitment consultant.

How will you apply it?

The final stage is to identify how you are going to apply the learning. Having great insight is one thing, but it's not much use to you if it stays in your head. Here's where you convert it into practical actions. What will you do with the insight you now have? Back to my example, here's what I decided: I will make a long list of potential questions for future interviews and identify my top three; I'll keep the longer list for if or when I'm offered the job; I will ask recruiters for specific feedback after each interview.

You can see that from even a small situation, there are things I have been able to take and apply. Although I failed to get that specific job, the interview ultimately helped me to become more successful in different ways. By taking time to reflect on times when we fail, we can grow stronger in our successes.

Summary

When we live through change there are going to be waves. We can't change that, but we can choose how we respond. In this chapter I've helped you to reflect on why it's hard to let go, as well as why failing at something doesn't make you a failure.

You now have specific practices to help you:

- Identify what no longer serves you
- Let go of the old
- Handle it when it doesn't work out
- Pick yourself back up
- Learn from your failures

Your ability to ride those waves has just increased exponentially!

Notes

Chapter 7:
How to Celebrate Success

Introduction

Wow! We've made such great progress. Whether you're celebrating the 'end result' or whether it's an interim step, congratulations! You might be feeling proud and recognising your accomplishments, or you might be thinking to yourself that I'm making a fuss over nothing. I've had times in my life where I've found it easy to celebrate and other times when it's felt almost impossible. I usually find it much easier to recognise the successes in other people than I do in myself. When I do manage to celebrate though, it seems to make the results last longer, and it also means I'm able to learn from what I've achieved, as well as from the things that haven't gone well. This chapter has lots of different activities you can try. I'm not for a minute suggesting you need to do them all. Take what works for you and see what else you can add to it. And if you want to challenge yourself, maybe pick the thing that seems to make you cringe and think, *I could never do that*. The chances are that there is learning in that for you.

Celebrations can look small or large. When I celebrated the first ten years of my business it was simply by having a nice dinner at home with my people. In fact, for the first few years of the business, every time we had a business birthday, I sent a packaged-up afternoon tea to my core team. It was a simple way to acknowledge what we'd achieved, and I looked forward to those little scones and sandwiches each year! The arrival of that box was the reminder to stop, look back at the year and see what we'd achieved. It wasn't actually about the cakes. It was about the tangible sign to take time to reflect. And I know it's not always easy.

Why it sometimes feels hard to celebrate

Are you a super celebrator or a reluctant recogniser of your own successes? Do you find it easy to notice what you've achieved, or are you constantly looking at what you could have done better or differently? People tend to fall into one of those two groups. Some people seem to find it easy to acknowledge success, celebrating often and in style, from dinners to celebrate professional achievements, to making a big deal about completing things. Other people find it much harder to notice and celebrate their own successes. I'm definitely the latter. They often get caught up in a sense of it not being quite good enough to recognise and mark what they've done. This is because of our own limiting beliefs and our experience of shame, the feeling of not being good enough. When we are constantly driving ourselves towards perfection, it can be almost impossible to recognise what we are achieving. If you struggle to recognise and acknowledge your own successes, you might want to do some work on understanding shame and vulnerability by looking at the work of Brené Brown in *Daring Greatly*™ and *Dare to Lead*™. I've seen every single time that I do this work in organisations how powerful it is to build our own shame resilience, so that the fear of not being good enough doesn't stop us from doing the things that we want to do.

How to recognise what you've accomplished and who you've become

I want you to take a minute and just stop. Take a deep breath in, and a slow breath out. You were, of course, already breathing. This is about becoming intentional about what's here for you right now. Allow yourself to recognise who you are in this moment. All that you have accomplished. Everything that you've achieved. From the beginning of time until now. Take it all in. Maybe you're being brave. Perhaps you've been taking on new projects and challenges recently. Or possibly you just learned how to do something that you couldn't do before. Or you're surviving a challenging situation. Some things might seem huge and significant, others small and trivial. Let it all flow through you, and notice who this wonderful human being is. You might find your breathing slows down a little, or even speeds up. You may even notice that your body feels different, or your thoughts start to change. And if you don't, that's fine. Simply paying attention to you, as the wonderful human being you are, is going to start to make a difference. I've done this in the past and it's sometimes brought me to tears. It's been such a new experience for me to actually stop and recognise what I've accomplished, rather than beat myself up for what I haven't done.

How often, if ever, do we take stock of what we've accomplished and, perhaps even more importantly, who we've become in the process? In the day-to-day hustle and bustle of life, we can lose sight of our achievements, minimise the challenges we've overcome and gloss over our own growth and development.

Over the years, I've worked with many, many clients who have struggled to notice their strengths and what they were capable of. One client in particular had chronically low self-belief. They struggled to see what they were good at, and kept pushing themselves over and over again to do and be more. I should probably add that I only work with coaching clients who are already successful, who are performing in their roles and where the organisation believes they have the potential for even more. So, I knew this individual was deeply skilled and capable as a senior leader, but in their eyes, they were never good enough.

Through our work together, we reached a point where I had a sense of some of their strengths. One day, I suggested we play a game. I invited them to create a list of twenty things that they were good at. I even offered to help – for every five that they came up with, I would add one to the list. It was like pulling teeth. You would have thought that I had asked them to name which of their friends they were willing to send to execution first. We sat, in pained silence, as my client racked their brain for things that could possibly count as strengths. There was an awkwardness. They fidgeted in their seat. Their eyes darted from side to side, as if they were scanning the room for potential threats. This was not easy. It had to be taken in their own time. Unable to even make eye contact with me, slowly, they started to identify small things. They were good at making the dinner. They could wrap gifts well. (Remember that this is a senior leader, running a part of an organisation and doing so skilfully and capably.) Maybe they were a good friend. Eventually, they got the first five down. I added one myself, something bigger, a more all-encompassing success. Over the course of an hour and a half, we created a list of twenty things together. Written on a scrap piece of paper, my client tucked the list into the back of their iPad cover. It stayed there for months. A dog-eared reminder of their strengths, taken out and reread as a way to soothe their soul and remind them that they were, in fact, good enough.

Could today be the day you start your own list? Do you already have one somewhere? No matter how small or large, begin by writing down what you're good at. What are the things that other people come to you for? What's something you've done for a long time? Which are the things that you can do without even really thinking about them? Start with your natural strengths, and write them all down. And if this feels almost impossible, ask one of your support squad for help. Ask them for three things you're good at. I'm sure they'll be delighted to help. Maybe you could offer to do the same for them? It somehow always feels easier to see strengths in others than it does in ourselves.

- I am good at...
- I find it easy to...
- People ask me to...
- I'm known for...
- I've always been able to...

You might find this very challenging. If you do, be kind to yourself. Start small. Take it one step at a time. If you need to come back to it tomorrow or the day after, that's okay. If it helps to write on scraps of paper or sticky notes, do that. Or make voice notes on your phone if you find it works to speak it rather than write it down. For me, when I've struggled the most, it helps to write it on scraps of paper. It's almost like it doesn't count if I write it like that. And it does get easier. I promise it gets easier. And we do this, because when we know what our strengths and achievements are, we can build on them. We can tackle more change in our lives, and we know what resources we have to draw on. That in itself gives us access to more that can help us in the future.

> When we know what our strengths and achievements are, we can build on them

It's also important to pay attention to the 'what' and the 'how'. The 'what' is the thing that you've achieved. The 'how' is what it took from you to achieve that. So, if you've found the new job, you celebrate getting the job. This is the 'what' that you've achieved. And it's vital to celebrate the fact that you were brave enough to step out of your comfort zone to look for a new job; you were clear on what you wanted; you showed skills in the interview process; and you stopped to think about how it fitted with the rest of your life. Whatever it takes to achieve the end goal is just as much worthy of celebration. That's where the true learning and growth comes from.

How to capture what you have learned through change

Celebrating your successes through change is one thing. Truly recognising what you've learned and discovered about yourself is another. When we face change we choose, or change we don't, we grow through the process. In pushing our own boundaries beyond our known day-to-day limitations, we are also developing ourselves. It can be helpful to take the time to understand what's different in us so that we can use it to inform and influence our future. Let's imagine that you have just been through some significant change – perhaps you've started a new relationship, or you've had a bereavement. It might seem odd to stop and look at what's changed in you now. But if we never actually recognise what we've learned, we can keep being presented with the same lessons over and over again.

> In pushing our own boundaries beyond our known day-to-day limitations, we are also developing ourselves

Today I'm inviting you to stop and reflect on your insight and new-found wisdom about yourself as a result of a recent change. If you're still in the thick of it, bookmark these pages and come back to them in the future. On the other hand, if there's a change that happened within the last twelve months and you haven't taken stock of your learning, let's do that now.

Whenever I complete coaching with clients, I invite them to get clear on what they've learned and what they've discovered about themselves. I also invite all of my clients to do this at the end of the year. It seems like a natural point to reflect and decide what we want to take forward into the new year. Even though I do this process myself every single December, it never ceases to amaze me how much I can learn in the course of just living my life over a twelve-month period. The following reflection prompts can be used at the end of the year or when you're looking back at a specific change. Allow yourself to linger over these and to write down or record in some way what comes up for you.

Ten reflection prompts to identify your learning:

- What have I learned about myself?
- What have I relearned about myself?
- What was my biggest discovery?
- What surprised me?
- Who have I become through this?
- Which part of me is growing the most?
- What have I been able to let go of?
- Where am I still holding on to something that doesn't serve me?
- Where have I gained the greatest support?
- What's been my biggest challenge?

How to discover what's possible for you now

Once we've discovered what we've learned, and comprehensively recognised what's here now, we can start to look at what's possible for us next. Think of it like a spiral staircase. As the months go by, we end up facing similar challenges, situations and life events, but we do so from a different perspective. Even when we think we are going in circles, we have an elevated viewpoint. We may be engaged in the same things, but with new-found knowledge, skills and resources

> I was gripped by an intense fear that I was going to be judged if I put myself out into the wider world

to draw on. You might be faced with change that looks similar on the outside, but inside you will handle it differently. Equally, there may be proactive changes you want to make in your life, which you've previously held back from, scared to try or lacking in confidence or conviction. With the lessons you've learned from recent change, you might now feel more able to take those first steps.

When I first launched the Kirsty Maynor website, I was terrified. My jaw felt permanently clenched. I wasn't sleeping well. I was probably more short-tempered and less tolerant than normal. I was gripped by an intense fear that I was going to be judged if I put myself out into the wider world. 'I don't even own concealer,' was my statement, out of the blue, on the car journey to school the week before this website went live.

As might be expected, with no context or precursor conversation, my then fifteen-year-old daughter Scarlet replied, 'Huh?'

'I don't even own concealer!' I repeated. 'And if I go live with www.KirstyMaynor.com people will see my pictures, and they'll say nasty things about the bags under my eyes. I'm not sleeping great; it's a pandemic; and I've got bags under my eyes. I don't even own concealer!'

With the quick-minded directness of a fifteen-year-old, Scarlet looked at me sideways and said, 'Well, it's not as if you're world-renowned anyway.' Count on a teenager to keep your ego in check when you need it. Just as I was starting to draw breath and realise that she might have a point, she then also quickly added to her Brownie points by saying, 'And if they're saying that it's just because they haven't got anything else to do. Plus, if they're looking at your eyes, it's because you have nice eyes.' Crisis averted, thanks to Scarlet (and thank you for the compliment).

So, here's the thing – the site is live. I still have bags under my eyes, and I launched the site anyway because, ultimately, my mission was bigger than my fear of being judged. I am not perfect – I will never be perfect – but I can still create change. So, if there's something getting in the way for you, like not owning concealer, don't let it. Find your own Scarlet – be your own Scarlet – but take the steps regardless.

Fast forward a year, and I was much more comfortable with letting people see me, for the sake of helping them live through change in their own lives. I started to do things I never would have dreamed of. I did live sessions on Instagram – where there is no editing! – and I participated in a USA national publicity summit where I met with more than seventy media professionals in a sort of speed-dating situation. I had two minutes to pitch to them with my ideas for articles, radio features and TV clips. There is no way I could have done that without the experience I had when my website went live. In 2021 I delivered a live keynote speech to an audience of five thousand people even though it terrified me!

What I have been able to do since then was directly influenced by my experience with getting the website out there.

Now it's time for you to start to think about what's possible for you. Perhaps you didn't choose the change that came your way, but you've learned through it anyway. I know I learned so much about myself from losing my mum, although it's a change that I would have done anything possible to stop. I learned how much love means, how to make the most of each day, how to face the most devastating news with courage, and much more besides. I feel capable of more, having lived through that experience, and I know that, whatever change you have gone through, you too are now capable of more.

Make some time and space, perhaps go for a walk, and handle yourself gently as you pay attention to what's possible now. Even when you've not 'succeeded' at what you've faced, you will still be capable of more. Notice that now, and find a way to record it. It might inspire your next goals or future dreams. Take time to capture that now, while it's still in your thoughts.

In the last section, you reflected on your learning. Now we're going to do more journalling on what's become possible because of that learning. You are accessing some of the thoughts that would otherwise stay deep inside your head. When you write them down or pull them out of your mind into a voice note, or anything else that's tangible, you give yourself more to work with. You might start to notice patterns or realise something that you weren't aware of before. In co-active coaching, we talk about the balance of 'deepening the insight' and 'forwarding the action'. This is deepening your insight. It's helping you to learn more about yourself so that when you are doing things, they're more likely to be resonant and to have a longer-lasting impact. The prompts are general enough that you can use them for a specific change or for your life more widely – make them work for you, for what you need now.

Ten reflection prompts on possibilities:

- I can now...
- I believe that I...
- I know that...
- I am ready to...
- I want to...
- It's my time to...
- What's here for me now is...
- From the outside I now seem more...
- From the outside I now seem less...
- The biggest possibility for me now is...

Some of these prompts will seem similar – that's intentional. It can be helpful to just give yourself a set amount of time – even three minutes for each prompt is plenty. Then, when you have completed all the prompts, notice if there are themes emerging that might give you a sign towards something significant.

How knowing your love language can help you celebrate in your style

Once you've realised that you've got something to celebrate, the question is, how will you mark the occasion? You might not be used to celebrating successes in your life, but the chances are you have celebrated birthdays, anniversaries or big milestones. And sometimes it might not have felt like a celebration.

Have you ever celebrated something, only for it to not feel quite like the celebration you imagined? It could be that you've not quite lined up the way you've celebrated with your own preferred love language. There are a few different models of love languages, the ways we know that others love us. We might express our love for other people differently, but typically, our preferred love language is the way in which we know that those near to us care about us deeply. My suggestion is that by taking time to reflect on how you know you are cared about, you can use your preferred love language towards yourself. So, if you realise that your primary love language is gift-giving, you might choose to celebrate by buying yourself something small. Whereas if you discover that quality time is what matters more to you, it might feel more celebratory to give yourself a special day off. Which of these is the way you are most likely to feel loved?

It's most meaningful to me when someone I love:

- Gives me a hug = Touch
- Gives me a small present = Gift-giving
- Spends time with me = Quality time
- Sends me a note saying what they admire about me = Words of affirmation
- Does something practical to help me out = Random acts of kindness

Feel free to add your own thoughts on how you know you are valued and cared for. These are only starters. I don't believe that the five love languages are the only ways in which we know we are loved, or indeed that they work for everyone.

My main love language is words of affirmation. Gift-giving and touch are probably close joint second, but words of affirmation do make me feel loved. So, I love to receive cards that say nice things to me, or about me. It might seem like a tiny thing, but a text from someone to say what they appreciated gives me a much rosier glow than any lavish gift would ever do. Now that I know that, I can do things to celebrate which make me feel good. I might even write myself a note and keep it somewhere. Or find quotes that say things and use them as my phone home screen. The more you know about what matters to you, the more you can act on it.

In the next section, I'll share suggestions for ways to celebrate which line up with each of the love languages. For now, you might want to think back to previous times when you've celebrated. What do you notice about how you celebrated? Did it feel like it was meaningful to you? Give yourself full permission to celebrate your way. Only you know what genuinely feels like a celebration!

Understanding love languages can also be helpful if you have children and want to make sure you acknowledge their achievements in a way that feels good to them. You can work out what their primary love language is and then celebrate accordingly. I've even used it with leaders in organisations to help them think about different aspects of staff recognition programmes. Use it as a starting point, not a constraint.

How to celebrate in fifteen ways

Here are fifteen ideas to get you started – I'm sure you'll think of many more! You might also need to experiment with ideas to see what feels the most meaningful. This doesn't need to be an expensive thing either. In fact, it's usually more about the thinking behind the celebration. My daughter had a great conversation with family friends at dinner about this recently. She and one of our friends both talked about the importance of quality time, and that it's about the other person being intentional in spending time with you. For both of them, it wasn't important what they did with the time, it was important that the time was planned, and that the other person was fully present and not distracted. Try some of these and see what you notice. Does it feel like a celebration or just a thing that you've done? Do you feel you are truly appreciating yourself?

Touch

- Book a massage
- Give someone a hug or hug yourself (it might sound odd – try it!)
- Have a DIY facial or foot massage night

Gift-giving

Ideas for this love language are probably more obvious, though remember that it can be the smallest of gifts if this is your primary love language. Things that last will also make good choices because you'll remember that you gave yourself the thing in celebration of something specific. Small things that are significant to you will also matter.

Random acts of kindness

- Do something nice for yourself
- Make yourself a nice lunch
- Rearrange a room or a part of your house

Quality time

- Take a long lunch break from work
- Go for a run or a long walk, especially in the middle of the day
- Have an early night with a good book

Words of affirmation

- Write yourself a letter saying what you most appreciate about yourself and send it to yourself
- Pick one phrase or sentence that sums up what you're proud of and get it made into wall art or even a piece of jewellery or a key fob
- Record a voice note acknowledging your strengths and listen to it daily for a month

Summary

Many of you will have found this a big chapter – it's got a lot in it which can push you to thinking about when, where and, most importantly, how you celebrate success. You've reflected on why it's not always easy to celebrate and, particularly in the context of change that life throws at you, that there are still things to pay attention to. I hope you've found ways to acknowledge what you're achieving, and who you're becoming in the process. If you want to take this even further you can experiment with Colin Sprake's suggestion in *Entrepreneur Success Recipe* and 'Celebrate as if it has already happened', meaning to start something already experiencing the success and the benefit that will bring to others.

You've now got tips at your disposal for how to:

- Recognise what you've accomplished
- Capture what you've learned
- Discover what's possible for you now
- Know what your love language is and how it can help you celebrate
- Celebrate in different ways!

Notes

There Are Big Waves,

Eleanor Farjeon, *The Children's Bells*

There are big waves and little waves,

Green waves and blue,

Waves you can jump over,

Waves you dive thro',

Waves that rise up

Like a great water wall,

Waves that swell softly

And don't break at all,

Waves that can whisper,

Waves that can roar,

And tiny waves that run at you

Running on the shore.

Notes

PART 4

THE UNTANGLERS

Notes

Chapter 8:
Overcoming Barriers to Change

Introduction

Anyone who's ever faced change before, regardless of the person, irrespective of the context, knows that at some point there comes a point where you can't, won't or don't want to go forward. No matter how compelling the change in the first place (and let's face it, some changes that are thrown at us aren't even compelling to start with), we simply stall, freeze or get stuck somewhere, and it seems like any attempts at moving forward are futile.

This chapter explains the different barriers you're likely to face, what's sitting underneath those barriers, and gives you strategies to overcome them. It might surprise you to know that they actually tend to share their foundations with each other. A bit like the children's book *We're Going on a Bear Hunt* by Michael Rosen, there are different strategies for the things that get in the way. Being equipped with them now, before you actually need them, will help you to keep moving and make it less likely that you'll get stuck for longer than necessary. Because it does sometimes need to happen that you get a little bit slowed down along the way. Resistance strengthens your resolve to keep going. When you hit a barrier, you need to recommit to the overall aim of your change, and that helps you to know you are on the right track. And yes, it still sucks, but you do know you're heading the right way. These barriers can also get in the way of responding to change that life throws at us in ways that feel authentic and right. When we find ourselves out of integrity as we face the loss of our job, a bereavement or the ending of a relationship, it's usually because of these barriers. For each of them I'll help you discover what's causing the barrier, the impact it has and how to overcome it. By the end of this chapter you'll be equipped to handle:

- Fear
- Shame
- Confusion
- Inertia
- Lack of prioritisation

Fear

'I'm scared. Bad things are likely to happen'. Elizabeth Gilbert writes about creativity, and she talks about the role that fear will always play. If you view change as a creative pursuit – the act of creating your new future – then of course, it is inevitable that fear will play a role. Because when we cannot predict what happens next, there is always an element of edginess, of unease. To create the future, we need to let go of the present. And most people find that hard, at least to some extent.

> To create the future, we need to let go of the present. And most people find that hard

Sometimes, therefore, we stall because we're scared. We set out with good intentions, our vision is clear, and somewhere along the way, we encounter something that reminds us of the future uncertainty, and we stop. Frozen to the spot by the knowledge of what's unknown. We may be looking at changing jobs or careers and realise we don't know if we actually want what we're moving towards, or whether it will, in fact, be more fulfilling or rewarding than what we already have. Perhaps we're on a path of change to do with our family and relationships, and again, we realise that we don't have certainty about where we are heading or what will happen along the way, because of course, we never do. That fear, that realisation, that piece of change that had possibly been hidden until now, when it shows its face, is powerful. So powerful, in fact, that sometimes it's enough to stop the change forever. Or at least for a very long time. I'm thinking now of writers who set out to write books and then stall with fear, only to resume their creative endeavour years later when, potentially, the grip of fear has weakened or diminished, or the mission has grown around it. Fear has stopped me from having challenging conversations when relationships haven't been working. It's held me back from doing what I wanted to do. It's convinced me that I'm better off to stay with how things are.

So how do we tackle fear? What helps us to overcome this barrier?

Turn around and face it. Fear loses its power when we acknowledge its existence. It may still be there, but it ceases to control you.

In 2014, I decided I'd have a whole year of facing fear head on. It was a sort of crazy decision to be honest, and it was certainly scary! But I knew I had to do something to stop the apprehension and, at times, terror, from limiting my choices and the life I wanted to live. I'm not talking about fear of physical things, just to be clear. I'm talking about the fears of 'what if' or the imaginings of all the bad things that would happen, things people would say, or ways

I could fail. I made the choice that every time I felt myself feeling that familiar sensation, I would turn around in my head and walk towards it, instead of running away, scared. As I did so, the fear seemed to shrink. Making the dentist appointment I didn't want to make; calling the tax people to sort out a problem, even though I was convinced it would be horrible; or telling a close friend that I didn't want to do the thing that I'd promised to do. It all felt less daunting. From a distance, when I was usually glancing over my shoulder and running away, fear seemed enormous, solid and terrifying – definitely a thing to be avoided. But when I turned around and faced it, holding my nerve as it moved closer, it seemed to shrink, fade and become less consequential. It never disappeared completely, but it just lost its power over me. I was able to keep going with the things that I wanted, or needed, to do.

So, when fear is the thing that's stopping you, turn round and face it. Say it out loud if you want: 'I see you, fear, and I'm going ahead anyway.' I love this passage from *Big Magic* by Elizabeth Gilbert. It's a great metaphorical reminder of the choices we have about how we handle fear:

Dearest Fear,

Creativity and I are about to go on a road trip together. I understand you'll be joining us, because you always do. I do acknowledge that you believe you have an important job to do in my life, and that you take your job seriously. So, by all means, keep doing your job, if you feel you must. But I will also be doing my job on this road trip, which is to work hard and stay focused. And creativity will be doing its job, which is to remain stimulating and inspiring. There's plenty of room in this vehicle for all of us, so make yourself at home, but understand this: Creativity and I are the only ones who will be making any decisions along the way. I recognize and respect that you are part of this family, and so I will never exclude you from our activities, but still, your suggestions will never be followed. You're allowed to have a seat, and you're allowed to have a voice, but you are not allowed to have a vote. You're not allowed to touch the roadmaps; you're not allowed to suggest detours; and you're not allowed to fiddle with the temperature. Dude, you're not even allowed to touch the radio. But above all else, my dear old familiar friend, you are absolutely forbidden to drive.

Having lived with anxiety (and also depression) at points in my life, I would add that if it feels like your fear is having a disproportionate impact on your life and is stopping you or holding you back, it might be helpful to contact a professional such as a suitably qualified, experienced and accredited therapist or psychologist. Fear and anxiety are normal parts of being human, but they don't have to keep you a prisoner in your own life.

Top tip: face your fear (and ask for help if you need it).

- ➤ What are you scared of?
- ➤ What if that wasn't true?
- ➤ What becomes possible if you face that fear?

Shame

'I'm not good enough. I don't deserve to be happy'. This is the most painful of the barriers, because it's the sense that you're not good enough. That snarling voice in your head that stops you from living the life you are truly here to live. Closely related to fear, because it is effectively a fear of disconnection, is the feeling of shame. As Brené Brown describes in her work, shame is the deeply painful feeling of not being worthy of love and belonging. The sense of not being good enough. The belief that we are a mistake, not that we've made a mistake. And that belief or sense that we are not good enough – in many different ways – is enough to stop us as we move through change. I felt it when I was writing, the sense of not being clever enough to write a book, the fear of not being academic enough or popular enough or even, on my bad days, articulate enough. It would stop my fingers reaching the keyboard. In a stealth move, it would see my days filled with other things. It didn't want me to succeed because that might then make it redundant.

Shame drives disconnection. It loves being in a darkened room, crawling across the floor, and will make you feel like you don't deserve to achieve the change you're setting out to achieve. If you're setting out to start a new business, or you want to make changes to your health and physical fitness, even an ounce of shame is going to stop you in your tracks. Feeling like we're not good enough, that we don't deserve to be here, is excruciating and, sadly, it's part of our human existence. Brené's research has shown that the only people who don't experience shame have sociopathic tendencies. So, at some point in your living through change, the chances are you're going to have some shame lurking around.

As a certified facilitator of Dare to Lead™ I've helped thousands of people to learn about what shame feels like in their bodies, so that they can recognise the early signs and take the right steps to limit the impact it has. When we learn how to handle shame and build shame resilience, we don't stop ourselves from feeling shame, but it has a lesser effect. Just as I explained about fear, we don't lose the feeling of shame, but we reduce the power it has over us.

So how do you know when you're in shame? The same way we all feel the physical sensations of fear differently, the cues that you're experiencing shame are different for us all, but there are some similarities. You might notice that you feel hot and flustered, or that you get a dry mouth, or that you just wish the ground would swallow you up. One way to identify your own shame cues is to think of a time when you felt not good enough. Maybe you said something and then felt completely stupid, not smart enough. Or maybe you did something with your kids and felt not patient enough. Try and reconnect with what was going on in your body at the time and how you felt – those are the ways you know that you're experiencing shame. For me it's the way I feel when my jaw clenches, my legs feel heavy but energised, and I just want to get out of there. Usually, my cheeks get hot too and my eyes start to sting. When I feel like that, I know I need to take some time out, breathe and connect with another supportive human being, despite my brain screaming at me to do anything other than that.

For the context of this book and living through change, the key thing is to recognise when you're experiencing shame and then to reach out to someone you trust and tell them how you are feeling, even though that will be the last thing you want to do. Shame thrives on solitude, remember; it doesn't want you to reach out and tell someone what's going on. That's the equivalent of turning the light on and the monsters under the bed are no longer there. Reaching out, turning the light on, reminds you that you are not alone and builds connection. Which is exactly what the shame is trying to convince you that you're not worthy of.

Top tip: call your close friends.

- ➡ What are your strengths and best qualities?
- ➡ What if you already are good enough?
- ➡ Who's your best source of support when you feel that you're not good enough?

Confusion

'I don't know what I want'. Sometimes we realise that we don't actually know what we want or where we're going. And then it's oh-so-easy to stall. Imagine looking for a new job – you maybe get a couple of interviews and don't get the roles you hoped for. You might find you stop applying for other roles, start to settle back into your current job. Maybe you even wonder if you want to change jobs after all? I've been stopped by this barrier more times than I care to count. In fact, for several years I found it almost impossible to listen to what I wanted or needed, let alone to articulate it to myself or anyone else. I had tuned out my inner wisdom, and I just felt confused.

When I see clients facing this type of barrier, it's often because they've lost their clarity about what they're going for, and what's important to them – perhaps they never actually fully identified it in the first place. I call this a sense of false goals or false destinations. It's not that they don't seem real, but like a false partition wall, the real wall, or goal in this case, is actually behind what we initially see. In fact, it's why I start work with clients facing career transition, not by exploring what kind of job they want, but by exploring what matters to them. It might be that they think they want a job as a finance director or in a particular industry sector, but when we start to explore the bigger picture of what's important to them, we might discover a whole variety of roles that interest and excite them. If they start off just down the path of looking for another finance director job, they might end up hitting the barrier of confusion or lack of clarity.

You'll know this is the barrier you're facing if you find yourself doubting and questioning what you actually want or if you are tempted to, or actually, give up. When you start finding yourself thinking *I'm not sure what I'm doing* or *why am I even bothering?*

or even *what was I thinking?* It could be confusion. One word of caution on the last one: this could be a case of shame or lack of self-belief, so check in with yourself to see if the barrier feels more about the outside – the goal or circumstances – and less about the inside – you and your ability to achieve your change – before you continue treating it like confusion.

Once you're sure that the problem is that you're not sure (!), the solution is to get back to the beginning – go right back to the first chapters of this book and redo the activities to get clear on what you want, how it fits with the rest of your life, and what matters to you. You might even want to look at your values and how they can support you (see chapter 9). The chances are you might have skipped over some of those sections, or made assumptions about what was important to you, and not actually locked in the clarity about what you were doing. Pay attention to what comes up when you work through those sections of the book again and notice how much easier it is to keep going when you have that level of clarity.

Top tip: revisit your purpose.

- What is it you don't know, when you say 'I don't know what I want'?
- What does clarity give you?
- What if you did know what you wanted?

Inertia

'I can't be bothered'. I think of this as the 'can't be bothered' barrier. The sense that I just can't be bothered, that somehow the thing I thought was important has ceased to matter to me. Like the old me wanted to write a book, the me of today thinks scrolling through Instagram is a far better use of my time. And sometimes, this is a cover for other barriers that are deeper, but most of the time it's just a stalling tactic that our minds use to keep us from living a fulfilling life. I mean, I'm sure there are people who find it completely joyful to sit and scroll through social media for hours on end, but in reality, most people actually find greater meaning and a more resonant life in using their time to do other things. So how come, when we set our minds on some kind of change path, to create a difference in the way we live, inertia strikes? What is it that makes us grind to a halt on the thing that we long for and snuggle into the sofa instead? (Not that there is anything wrong whatsoever with snuggling, or sofas, or indeed social media, when chosen as a positive thing, rather than as a distraction from what we truly want.)

Partly, it's a way of avoiding failure or of our minds keeping us safe. If I never try to train for, and run, a marathon, then I can never *not* achieve it, so I'll just sit on the sofa instead. I might have decided that I want to start a business, have an idea for a product or service that I think is needed, but if I don't actually ask people if they want to buy it, I'm protecting myself from them saying 'no'. Partly, inertia can also be a way of lack of clarity manifesting itself, for which, see the previous section. Mostly though, when I work with clients who are not taking action towards the change they want to create, it's because they don't know how. And, linked to that, they believe that there is one right way or at least a small number of options.

> Stumbling forward, pretty much regardless of the action, is the only right way

The reality is that stumbling forward, pretty much regardless of the action, is the only right way. Because as long as you are sitting on the sofa, you're not getting any closer to the change you want to be living. But when you get up off the sofa and start to move, no matter which direction, you will get closer to what you long for. I can imagine some of you scratching your heads right now and thinking, *but what if I go in the wrong direction?* And the answer is that there is no wrong direction, not if you want to move towards your desired end goal. Because, ultimately, momentum will get you there. Yes, there might be quicker ways, shortcuts and paths that will accelerate the process, but as sure as the sun comes up in the morning, any movement is quicker than none at all. So, if you're starting a business then taking action, any action, is going to create momentum. If you're looking to redesign or reconfigure your house, taking action will get you closer. Sitting on your sofa scrolling Instagram will not get you closer.

Top tip: move your body.

- ➡ What's one thing you can do today to get moving?
- ➡ What would you do to help a friend get started if they were in your shoes?
- ➡ One year from now, what will you be proud of?

Lack of prioritisation

'I've got too much to do'. 'I'm just too busy' said nobody ever, when facing change. Oh wait, it's probably the number one excuse – I mean, reason – for not getting where you want to get to. You've seen all the memes, heard all the quotes. Everybody has the same twenty-four hours in the day, yes, even you. And yet, some people manage to achieve all kinds of things and others less so. There is nothing wrong with that whatsoever, as long as you are living the life you want to, and you're feeling fulfilled. But if you keep aiming for something and it doesn't ever happen because you never quite put it at the top of your priority list, it's time for you to reprioritise.

I am incredibly busy – I run a business, lead a team, am a single parent, have hobbies I enjoy and I'm also writing a book. And I still know that I just need to pick up my phone and I can instantly lose an hour. I'm embarrassed to admit how many hours I spend on my phone, and for you it might be your phone or TV or something else that isn't nourishing and energising you. When we prioritise what we want, we commit to it. Not twenty-four hours a day, I'm realistic about the rest of your life. But we set the intention that it matters, and our actions align with that intention. If you decide you want to learn to play the flute, buy yourself a flute and start to take lessons. But if for the rest of the week the flute sits in the case, you're probably not going to get much better. If you want to create a shift in your life and you don't put in the time and the energy, the chances are it just isn't going to happen. So, when you notice yourself always prioritising other things or other people, what can you do?

Firstly, I want you to get totally honest with yourself: do you believe you deserve the change you're trying to create? Honestly, truthfully, 100% - do you? Because sometimes the reason we don't prioritise ourselves and our goals is because we don't believe we deserve to have the nice home, be happy in our job or have a relationship that truly works for us. If that's the case, then the real barrier is self-belief, and I'm going to invite you to pause right here and point you to the sections on self-care and self-compassion in Chapter 9. Until you have at least a smidgen of belief in yourself and your worth, you will always struggle to prioritise what you dream of, and you'll keep putting yourself at the bottom of the pile.

Secondly, if you're still here and you do believe you deserve the change, it's time to alter the core beliefs you have about what it means to prioritise you and your change. Prioritising you does not mean ignoring everyone else and excluding all other priorities. It doesn't have to be your sole priority, but it does have to be on the list, ideally at, or close to, the top. I happen to believe that if you have a job and any form of significant other relationships on the go – family, partner, parents or friends – you will always have multiple priorities. You may never have the single-minded pursuit of a sole focus, in the way that some people can. But we can, and we should, include ourselves on the list, and not just at the bottom, with only the scraps of time and energy left over. Think of when you make gingerbread cookies.

> Prioritising you does not mean ignoring everyone else and excluding all other priorities

You roll out the dough, cut out the shapes, gather what's left up and roll it again to make some more. If you're lucky, you get a couple of rolls, and then you have the last piece that you can maybe use to make one or two final cookies. Those last ones might feel good – you eked out the last of the dough. But they never taste as good; the texture is more likely to be overworked; and you know that the ones from the first roll are much tastier. It's the same with you and your energy and resources for change. You need to make sure whatever you're aiming for is in the first rolling of the day. Make time for you; take the steps you need to when you have your most energy; don't leave yourself until last. Yes, I know that when you serve the dinner, you give the kids their choice of the roast chicken or pie serving, but this is your life. Prioritise you. They'll still get pie; it will still be tasty. But you need to put yourself and your change higher up the list and believe that you deserve it.

Top tip: trust yourself

- ➡ Which of the rubber balls do you need to drop? (See change myth and change reality 7 in Chapter 1.)
- ➡ What's it worth to prioritise yourself?
- ➡ Who can help you to put yourself higher up the list of priorities?

Summary

Barriers to change will occur. You now have the tools to handle them so that they don't completely stop you in your tracks. Here's a short reminder for easy reference. You might even want to write these on a sticky note, or I've got downloadable cards that you can print at home at www.untangledbook.com

Barrier	Key Reminder
Fear	Face your fear
Shame	Call your friends
Confusion	Revisit your purpose
Inertia	Move your ass!
Lack of prioritisation	Trust yourself

Chapter 9:
Discovering Change Skills

Introduction

What are the core skills we need to live through change? And why are we never taught them at school?!

Most people think you're either good at handling change or you're not, based on some divine destiny or your combined life experiences. In fact, many parents confidently state that their child doesn't cope well with change, even before they can reach things off a countertop. The reality is that living with, coping with and thriving through change is a set of skills that you can learn at any age and there is a core set of tools that will help you along the way.

There was a time in my life when I thought I knew all of those tools. I felt confident that I could handle whatever changes life threw at me. I'd moved house thirteen times by the time I was fifteen. I went to two primary schools and two secondary schools. It became a family joke that if you had carpets, curtains and lightshades, the house was done. My parents were great at seeing opportunities. A new

> Living with, coping with and thriving through change is a set of skills that you can learn

house or a new job. A business venture. A new chapter. Some of those opportunities worked out well. They both had successful careers in education. We all learned a lot and became good at coping with change – at least on the surface. We made new friends. We thrived at school. We laughed together. Some of their adventures were less successful. Their business failed within eighteen months, leaving my parents bankrupt. When I was aged eleven, it felt like we had lost everything, and in some ways we had. We moved to the middle of nowhere. A cottage called Eagle's Nest, which tells you how remote it was. When my mum first lit a fire, water ran down the walls inside the house. It was home. And it was filled with love. But we needed to change, and fast. I learned from that. So, as an adult, I thought I knew how to handle change. I had formalised my lived experience with professional training in change management. It was even on my business cards. I was a change management consultant for one of the big four consultancy firms. Companies paid big money for me to tell them how to plan and communicate change in their organisations. I had PowerPoint documents showing pretty change curves. I could tell you how to implement new systems and make sure that people used them. I knew my stuff.

Then one day, it all came crashing down. I lost my job. The proverbial hit the fan. Called into a meeting room two weeks before Christmas, I had no idea what was about to happen. Hearing the words didn't even feel real. Maybe I was dreaming. If so, it was a nightmare. Fear and devastation grabbed me in a headlock. I ran out of the room to the ladies' toilets. Thankfully, they were close. I struggled to catch my breath. I had done nothing wrong, but my working world had just ended without warning. I was the sole earner in a household. My husband and daughter needed me to find a new job and fast. What would I do now? But there was a massive problem – I had lost all faith in myself. I believed I was nothing without the big brand behind me. I felt desperate, lost and completely incapable of dealing with the uncertainty. I didn't even know who I was without my professional identity.

What turned it around for me was when I decided that I was the one who was going to determine what happened next. This time it was truly up to me. I realised that the change had to start from inside. I couldn't fix this with a new suit to wear to work (yes, I wore suits in those days!). I couldn't go on a course to discover the person at my core. I had to take a long, hard look at who I was and what mattered to me. I needed to find my own self-belief. To know that my value comes from who I am, not what I do or the job title on my business card. My next steps would need to be to do the work on my mindset and to develop the inside skills to carry me forward. Those skills helped me to find my next job, rebuild my confidence on stronger foundations and, ultimately, create my own award-winning business helping others to do the same. Those skills I thought I had were replaced with those I truly have. The ones with which I can live through any kind of change. I'm going to let you into a secret. These are the kinds of skills that make you look like a ninja warrior when you use them in your everyday life. People will see you riding the waves of change that life throws at you, making bold moves as you launch yourself into new ventures and generally thriving. Friends and co-workers will wonder aloud how you do it. The truth is that these skills are straightforward to learn, especially when you take them step by step, as we're about to do. But they're not easy for others to copy when you use them together. Like a good recipe, the basics are simple; it's how you use them in combination that makes the real difference. And you don't need to work through them all in sequence. Start with the skills that are most helpful for you now.

By the end of this chapter, you'll have the frameworks to help you with:

- Finding your purpose
- Honouring your values
- Practising self-care
- Living with self-compassion
- Becoming friends with vulnerability
- Discovering your courage

Finding your purpose

'Purpose, it's that little flame, that puts a fire under your ass'. (*Avenue Q.*)

We've already touched on this earlier when we put change in its bigger context, but living in alignment with your purpose is also a core skill. Living without purpose is living without basis. You'll find it hard to hook into anything, to stay the course and to have something to anchor off.

Knowing your purpose helps you to answer the question 'for the sake of what?' about many aspects of your life. What's the reason for you getting up in the morning? What's the life you want to live? What's your purpose?

This might be ultra-clear. Or it might be a new question. And the reason it matters in the context of navigating change is that you are always working in a bigger context. Whatever kind of change you are facing, it's part of a much bigger picture. If you know what your purpose and your values are, then you can make choices about how to live through change that align with those.

How about you? What's your purpose? What is the reason you're here? One easy way to start to connect with your purpose is to start to think about the threads that have been woven throughout your life for a long time. And remember that it doesn't have to be a big, world-serving purpose (though it can be!). It can be a small, perfectly formed purpose. Maybe you're here to be happy and to share that happiness with those you meet. Maybe your purpose is about bringing the gift of love. Maybe it's about leaving the world a better place in some specific way. What's the reason you get out of bed?

With coaching clients, I sometimes do a visualisation that can help you connect with your purpose. One part of it invites you to imagine that you are at your own eightieth birthday party. Friends, family and people who matter to you are sharing the difference you've made in their lives. Imagine what you'd want them to say. What would you want to hear?

> Let yourself listen to the tiny whisper or the giant roar in your heart

What difference would you want to have made? The chances are you are starting to connect with your overall purpose.

I've stopped and thought about this myself. I've also done other work on my purpose. I always come back to helping people to find the gift of self-belief. I want to live wholeheartedly with love, and I want to help people unlock their potential. I can do those things in lots of different ways. I ultimately want to have made a difference to my friends, family and clients and the people around them. For them to walk taller because I've been in their lives.

What's your purpose? Why are you here? And remember that you can't get this wrong. Let yourself listen to the tiny whisper or the giant roar in your heart.

Honouring your values

We all have core values. They guide us through tough choices, help us to live with integrity and are often the reason we get wound up about the same things over and over again. When we live in alignment with our values, we tend to feel more fulfilled, and we find decision-making easier. But when we are out of sync with those guiding stars, things feel off-centre, unbalanced, and it can be difficult to know what we want. This means that when we face change, it's vital that we know and understand our core values and that we live in ways that honour those. It's not always easy – in fact, once we know what our key values are, we can sometimes find ourselves facing challenges and even more change. Sometimes when we realise a value that matters to us, we recognise we need to take a different direction or shift things in the way we're living. However, even on the days when it's hard, knowing the things that truly matter to you is helpful.

So, what are values? A dear and trusted former member of my team, Zoe Hawkins, describes them as things you can't put in a wheelbarrow. I'm not quite sure why she chose that image rather than something more mundane, like a box or a purse, but there you go. Your values will not be found inside a wheelbarrow. They will be found instead inside in your heart and mind, because values are your guiding principles, the things that motivate you and matter to you most. Not in physical objects, more in ways of living and being. And they can be met in different ways. As an example, two of my core values are courage and authentic honesty. It matters to me to be real and to be brave – even when it's hard or I'm scared. I know that I'm being true to myself when I live up to those two values, and I also find it extremely difficult when I don't.

Values don't change over time; they're as consistent in you

as your own DNA. Like rainbows, some may shine more brightly than others at certain times in our life, but the colours are always there. And while, if you look at a list of values, you might want to have them all, if we are truly honest, we are guided by two or three core values at any one time. These are the things that help you make difficult choices, and that also absolutely matter if anyone cuts across them. In fact, one way of finding out some of your values is to think about what annoys you. Whatever it is, have a look at what sits underneath, and you'll probably find one of your core values. As an example, one thing that I cannot stand is people not telling the truth. I'd rather you tell me something awful that might potentially be hurtful than you lie about it. Looking under that, we don't have to go far to see that one of my core values is honesty. I was once in a work situation where someone senior in the organisation lied to me and about me. It shook me that they would go so far to protect themselves. I was stunned that someone could lie outright and say they had done something that they hadn't done. This wasn't my daughter saying she'd brushed her teeth when the dry sink showed the truth. It was a senior leader in an organisation saying that they had taken action that they hadn't. With huge consequences. In my eyes, not only is that person dishonest, but they are also cowardly. I will never work with them again. My values were crossed too far. And I'm lucky that courage is another top value for me. It isn't comfortable or easy to be honest. There are times when I would find it easier to be dishonest or to avoid the conversation. My values won't let me. It's hard but always worth it in the long term.

Another way that helps you to identify core values is to think about a mountain top moment, a time when you felt completely fulfilled. If you tell that story to someone else, the chances are they'll be able to hear your values loud and clear.

Once you know what your values are, the key is to not leave it at one-word answers but to fully explore what you mean by those. In the words of Brené Brown, you need to 'operationalise them'. This is vital in an organisational setting, where we need to set out what the values actually look like in specific behaviours and what behaviours are not in alignment with those values. It also holds true in our individual lives, where it can be helpful to get clarity on which behaviours demonstrate our values and which behaviours go against them.

Let's get specific. Complete the following sentences for each of your core values:

- ➥ I know I'm in alignment with this value when I...
- ➥ I know I'm on the slippery slope with this value when I...

This helps you become more equipped to recognise when you're not living in a way that's aligned with your values and when something might need to change. One way I know that I am not living in alignment with my value of courage, and am therefore likely to be short-tempered and feel frustrated with myself, is when I hold back from having those tough conversations. So, if I notice that I'm cranky, I can get curious about that. If I notice that I'm not having a conversation with someone, I can realise that I'm not being courageous and work out what I need to do to address that. I can also recognise the times when I am being courageous and how it feels to be aligned with that value (not that I want to be scared all the time, just that I want to be courageous when it's called for, and not shy away from things because I get scared).

In fact, the act of setting up my own brand called upon my courage, and I've been able to keep going because it's aligned with my purpose. I wanted to stay hiding behind the Firefly brand. I got completely panicked by the thought of being out in the public eye, seen and ready to be attacked. I felt like I was a gazelle, walking out into the middle of a plain and holding up a big sign saying 'Here lions, come and get me!'. I even started to worry that people would comment on the bags under my eyes. It was borderline ridiculous, but it was also real. I was scared. I didn't want to be criticised; nobody does. But to live courageously, I can't let that stop me. For those of you who are still struggling to identify your core values, you can find a list on my website to help you get started. And don't feel constrained by the list; use it as a springboard.

Do keep an eye out for what I call 'values aspirations' – the temptation to want to have all the values. It can happen particularly when you look at a list of values and you think, *oh yes, I want to have that as my top value.* This thinking often comes from what we believe to be socially desirable or acceptable. So, we might think that it would be great for one of our top values to be positivity. And for some people that genuinely is one of their core values – it will drive their actions and decisions and motivate them beyond almost anything else. But for most of us that's probably not top of the list and, if you looked at our past, present and future, you would see other values that are more significant to us.

Also, give yourself permission to get creative and make up a value. Another one of my values is magic sparkle – you won't find that one on a list, but to me, it's the absolute essence of wanting what I do and who I am to bring sparkle and zest. If things feel mundane or regular, then the chances are I'm not honouring that part of me.

Practising self-care

This next skill comes with a reminder that I believe in you and your potential. And I exist to help you live your life more fully and to thrive through change. I feel the need to underline that because this change skill is one that comes with tough love. It's the skill of self-care, and it's definitely one that many of us struggle with. In fact, I'd go so far as to say that lots of people care way more for others than they do for themselves. For generations, many of us have been trained, raised and guided to be the ones who care for others. And yet, it often comes with a huge cost, particularly when we are in the throes of change. We all know of friends and colleagues who've been dealt cards of change, only for it to be the thing that broke them. Job loss, bereavement, health changes, relationship changes or even the menopause can tip us over the edge. Bruised and hurt, we end up retreating further into a cave of our own creation, and it can take us a long, long time to emerge. And the alternative, where we are choosing to create significant change in our lives, can also bring us to a point of burnout, or even of questioning whether we want what we're pursuing in the first place.

I learned about self-care the hard way – I saw the opposite when I was growing up. My mum was a very strong woman, raised as a survivor and committed to doing her best in everything. Whilst she had her occasional indulgences and luxuries in the material aspects of life, she frequently pushed herself to breaking point by meeting the needs of others way before herself. To her, the concept of self-care was an anathema. I watched her push herself to breaking point repeatedly. She even told me outright that it was selfish to put what I wanted or needed first. She wasn't mean. It was all she knew. You put others first. Always. But when I developed reactive depression as a student, and when postnatal depression later grabbed me and tried to take me under, it was no longer an option for me. I needed to know different, to learn different. I didn't know how to actually care for myself.

When I was younger, I thought self-care was buying myself

small gifts or having a day doing something nice. I treated myself to spa days. I bought myself flowers, having never found a partner who would buy them for me (my ex-husband said that flowers were for 'special occasions'). When I saw a need, I met it. And part of me was satisfied, temporarily. Because that's the result of that kind of self-care. You give yourself a little boost; you potentially feel better for a day. But the benefit of that sugar-coated (did I mention the chocolates I bought?), superficial, glossy kind of self-care is not the kind of result you need to sustain you through change. It was nice, but it didn't change how I felt beneath the surface.

So, when my mum died suddenly, when I was faced with the pandemic and when I wanted to create major changes in my relationships, I stalled. I didn't know how to function. I felt completely and utterly lost. I literally didn't know how to go on. My self-care practices, as established as they were, no longer scratched the surface of what I needed. I needed genuine self-care. The kind of care that is hard to give yourself but that can be transformative. It was time to change what self-care looked like for me. And it was tough. It's easy to do the superficial self-care. The deep kind of taking care of ourselves is much harder. In reality, this stuff is hard, hence the tough love.

Buying myself flowers wasn't difficult (although I sometimes didn't feel I deserved them). But putting in place healthy boundaries and saying 'no' felt like a completely different ball game. Actually learning to put myself first and to believe, even partially, that this wasn't selfish, as I had been brought up to believe. That felt impossible at times, in fact, most of the time. But what I noticed was that it changed me, but not in the ways that I feared. I didn't become the Wicked Witch. I didn't ostracise people I cared about. Instead, I felt more grounded, more centred and more at peace.

> My ability to cope with change grew in direct proportion to my ability to truly care for myself

It sounds cheesy. It felt liberating. My ability to cope with change grew in direct proportion to my ability to truly care for myself. To be able to prioritise sleep, moving my body and making time for myself opened up a whole world of possibilities. That's important since these are ultimately what no one else can do for us. In fact, self-care is exactly that – it's the care for self that others can't do. Buying a new gadget? Someone else can do that. Booking a golf day? You can outsource that. But holding a boundary and not overcommitting yourself? That's up to you. And the flip side, nudging yourself to meet a friend for a drink when your anxiety makes you want to hide under the duvet? Again, you're it. It's not all hearts and flowers. In fact, it's rarely hearts and flowers. But it is sweet; it does taste good; and it is absolutely worth it. Take care of you. Exquisite care of you. You are the one thing you can (learn to) count on.

Make a start today by writing a list of ways in which you can take care of yourself. Here are ten prompts you might use to make that list a bit longer:

- Ask a friend for suggestions.
- Think about what someone you admire might try to do.
- What would you suggest to a child?
- What's the thing that could make the biggest difference?
- What's the thing you would be scared to do?
- What's the one thing that feels impossible but also super-helpful?
- What would you do if your life depended on it?

- What's the thing that feels so simple it almost feels silly?
- What would you do if you knew it would be guaranteed to work?
- What's the one thing your heart and soul needs?

Living with self-compassion

You might be thinking, *hang on, I just read about that*, but this is the skill of self-compassion. Although it's similar to self-care (both in the letters in the words and as a skill), it is in fact different, and I want to keep them separate. Self-care is the care for yourself that others can't do. Self-compassion is the way you talk to yourself in your head. Think of them as a pair of skills, with self-care being the practical things, self-compassion being more of the inside game. The leading expert on this is Kristin Neff, who has researched both the importance of self-compassion and the different parts of it. She describes these as the following:

- Self-kindness versus self-judgement
- Common humanity versus isolation
- Mindfulness versus over-identification

'At the most basic level, self-compassion simply requires being a good friend to ourselves. This is heartening news, because most of us already know how to be a good friend, at least to others.' (Kristin Neff, *Fierce Self-Compassion*).

Once upon a time, I was my own worst enemy. Life felt like an endless battle, only no one else could see it. Every minute of every day, my mind was criticising me. Listening to the soundtrack inside my head brought never-ending judgement and condemnation. According to that voice in my head, I was not good enough, smart enough, caring enough, quick enough, thoughtful enough... you get the picture. It was exhausting. I never got a break. From dawn to dusk, I spent my days trying to outrun that voice by attempting to be even better than the day before, but it was never enough. Until one day, I started to train as a facilitator of *Daring Greatly* with Dr Brené Brown and her team. They introduced me to the work of Kristin Neff and, with help from a psychologist, I slowly started to shift from what I jokingly called 'Demanding FM' to 'Compassion FM' inside my head. Imagine that the things that rumble around in your head all day are like radio stations. You get to choose what you listen to. I learned to recognise what types of situations prompted the radio dial in my mind to switch to Demanding FM (not a great station to be honest) and how to notice that was what was happening.

By doing that work, I was able to be more compassionate to myself. I started with small steps that had a big impact, like being less judgemental of myself and giving myself credit for what I was achieving, rather than criticising myself for what I wasn't. I started to practise self-kindness over self-judgement. It wasn't easy, but it was totally worth it. And even now, I still know I need to work at it. At times when I'm under pressure or feeling exposed, I know that the temptation will be for Demanding FM to start blaring in my head. I have to actively work to shift the dial to Compassion FM. To notice that the presence of Demanding FM is a sign that I need to slow down, take care of myself, and that there is probably something else going on that needs attention. It doesn't even need to be big things. I remember one early January day a few years ago, I was feeling stressed; start of the new year nerves had me pinned down. My to-do list was longer than my arm. I felt I'd never get it all done. Demanding FM said to sit at my desk at home on the 2nd January, the Christmas tree in the other room, lights twinkling with no one to see them. If I worked all day, started early and worked late, maybe I'd get it all done?

Compassion FM offered a different idea. How about we take the laptop, make a nice hot chocolate and curl up on the sofa in front of the tree? We could get the work done there. It doesn't have to be a punishment.

I listened.

I chose Compassion FM and I got everything done. Much quicker than I would have done if I'd chained myself to my desk.

For today I want to invite you to start to pay attention to the inner conversations you have with yourself. Ask yourself the following and write in your journal about what you discover:

- Which radio station are you listening to in your mind?
- What's the main soundtrack?
- What prompts you to listen to one station over another?
- How can you listen more to a different radio station in your mind that might be more supportive?

What might that give you?

The second part of self-compassion in Kristin Neff's model is common humanity. This is the antidote to the feeling of self-pity, the sense of 'why me?', which can often arise in situations when things feel difficult. When we are facing transition in our lives, or when we are trying new things and pushing the boundaries of our previous comfort zone, we can end up facing failure. If we can stop and realise that this is a common part of being human, that we do fail and face difficulties, we can prevent ourselves from falling into a trap of feeling it is only something that happens to us.

When we are living with change, we are pushing ourselves beyond the known, comfortable, safe and familiar world of our day-to-day lives and stretching into something new. That's challenging. It doesn't matter whether that's something we've chosen, like a new career path, starting a family or relocating, or something that's been thrust upon us like job loss, bereavement or relationship change. The ground beneath our feet is shifting, and our mind scrambles to try and keep us safe. Most of the time our brain regards the current reality as the safest place. Unless we are living with threat, the mantra seems to be 'stay with the status quo'. So, when we face change, the mind wants to resist and can get incredibly creative about how to do that. By paying attention to our thoughts and by noticing them without getting attached to them, we are able to stay more present with the reality. This is why the third part of self-compassion is about mindfulness. For which you don't need prayer beads, a yoga mat, or even to sit down. Though you can of course if you want to! At its simplest form, mindfulness is about noticing a thought, without getting caught up by it. There are tons of resources out there to help you learn about mindfulness and practise it. And I'm definitely not an expert, so I want to keep it simple.

> Most of the time our brain regards the current reality as the safest place

I used to resist mindfulness like my life depended on it – ironic, I know! My team at Firefly included mindfulness practitioners and even mindfulness teachers, and it took every ounce of restraint for me not to roll my eyes and run away when we used mini-mindfulness techniques with leadership teams we worked with on development days. To Sarah and Ivor, I apologise – I am a reformed character! In all seriousness though, I resisted the idea of mindfulness because it felt daunting and probably, if I'm completely honest, because I was scared I couldn't do it. (Anyone notice Demanding FM making an appearance?) Any time we sat or stood and someone said those fateful words, 'gently close your eyes and start to pay attention to your breathing', I panicked. Because any time I sat and paid attention to my breathing, I would notice the thoughts. And those thoughts were powerful. If the aim was to not have any (which it's not by the way), I was doomed! My mind was (and is, just like yours) a powerful thing. Trying to stop my thinking felt like trying to hold up an articulated truck with a feather. I simply couldn't do it. Attempting any mindfulness activity seemed to me to be the ultimate recipe for failure. But you see, I was wrong. Because mindfulness is something in which it is impossible to fail. Simply by pausing whatever else you're doing and paying attention, you're practising mindfulness. And that's the key. It's a practice. It's never complete. It's never finished. It's never wrong. You practise. Over and over and over again. It's like piano practice without a concert.

There is no performance.

This, dear friends, is what made it possible for me to start to practise mindfulness. Releasing myself from the pressure to get it right, perform or succeed has (on a good day) liberated me to

> Trying to stop my thinking felt like trying to hold up an articulated truck with a feather

practise mindfulness over over-identification. When I pause my daily stuff, and pay attention to my mind and my breathing, I notice thoughts and I can let them go. And slowly, over time, the space between the thoughts gets bigger. Yes, I still get distracted. 100%. And I still get hooked up in my own thinking and start to believe it's all real (what Kristin calls over-identification), but occasionally I do have glimmers of recognising that the thoughts are just thoughts. I don't have to believe them. I don't have to act on them. I can just let them pass on. So, for today, I'd like you to just experiment, practise, try it out. There are resources on my website to help you, but the most important thing is to find something that works for you. It could even be as simple as getting your shoes on and going for a walk, noticing the way your foot feels as it touches the ground and gradually slowing your pace by half and then by half again. Or lie on the floor and notice the way your breathing is today, the in-breath and the out-breath. You might end up with kids and pets joining you! Have it be simple. Let it be a gift to yourself. And see what shows up.

Becoming friends with vulnerability

Vulnerability is risk + uncertainty + emotional exposure (Brené Brown). It's the feeling in your stomach when you don't know what's going to happen, but it doesn't feel like it's going to be good. It's when you want to run away, hide or sometimes come out fighting. It's a feeling we're all familiar with, but most of the time we want to avoid it. And yet, it's a core part of facing change. In any situation where we are facing the unknown, it is inevitable that we will feel vulnerable – in both the small times and the big. You might notice it when you have a conversation with your boss about applying for a new job. You'll feel the tugging in your stomach when you tell your kids you're planning to move house, and I guarantee it will be present as you live your way through the agony of losing someone you love. We find it hard when we feel vulnerable and so we try to avoid it, cover it up or numb ourselves from the feeling. When I've faced big changes in the past, the knowledge that I have to face the vulnerability has almost always threatened to stop me in my tracks. It's been the thing that has kept the words in my mouth rather than saying them out loud. It's been what's kept me going round in circles rather than forging a new path. It's ultimately been the thing that has stopped me from making changes I wanted to make in my life. And the only way through it is to face it. Which sucks.

So how do we live with vulnerability? The answer is we do the thing that seems like madness. We defy all logic. We do the thing that has our mind screaming, *no, stop, don't do it*. We reach out. We connect with another human being. Even when it's the last thing in the world we want to do. Especially when it's the last thing in the world we want to do. The act of reaching out, connecting with someone else and sharing what's going on is enough to change things. Because it reminds us that we are not alone. And all the stuff we are making up in our heads, every story we are telling ourselves, each myth that's stopped us from facing our fears, they all get a new perspective. It may not be any more true or accurate than the views we already had, but it changes things. So, we reach out to someone who's earned the right to hear our story, and we tell them what's going on. And, with any luck, they offer us empathy in return.

Discovering your courage

You can't face change without courage. Because facing any kind of change is scary. People often think that being courageous is the absence of fear. But it's not. It's seeing the fear and walking towards it rather than turning and running the other way. Jack Canfield and Janet Switzer state this fairly directly. '*Some people will do anything to avoid the uncomfortable feeling of fear. If you are one of those people, you run an even bigger risk of never getting what you want in life. Most of the good stuff requires taking a risk.*' (The Success Principles). Both reactive and proactive change involve stepping into the unknown, and that's daunting. If it wasn't, we would all continually evolve, make bold moves in our lives and never hesitate to step into new ways of living. And sometimes we do, but let's be honest, not often. It's back to what I said about self-compassion. We get scared because our brains try to protect the status quo. But in the twenty-first century, there are all kinds of opportunities for change that mean we have to face those fears and tie ourselves to our courage. Where self-care and self-compassion go hand-in-hand, here we have another pair. Courage and vulnerability also pair up. Wherever you find one, you'll find the other. Because when we face our fears, we end up in a place of vulnerability. Vulnerability is the greatest measure of courage we have. And it sucks!

In the section on fear in Chapter 8, I talk about the year that I made a decision to run towards my fear rather than away from it. I simply decided that I wasn't going to let fear stop me. I would see it, and I would take it on – like a challenge. What opened up for me that year was a whole world of opportunities that I could never have imagined. I had to learn to trust myself and to remind myself over and over and over again that whatever happened, I would be okay. Because in reality, the things I was afraid of were not real. They were imaginary versions of the future, and I could just as easily create other imaginary versions in which everything worked out just fine. Either way, the only way to discover what would actually happen was to take the steps forward towards my fear.

Since I studied with Brené Brown that year, I have become so much more aware of where I want to, and need to, be more courageous in my life. It honestly is the gift that keeps on giving. Thankfully, I also have the skills now to help me. And I have a lot of evidence from my own life and my clients' that the thing we're scared of is rarely as tough as we think it is. Even when it feels huge and terrifying. Every aspect of my life is enriched by my courage.

It's evident in the small things and also in the conversations that take weeks and months to build up to. Sometimes we can even take years to tell our truth, until we find enough courage to face the fear.

I had been wanting to tell her for ages. I felt like I was living a lie. The truth sat inside me, but it never got out. It ate at me from the inside, clenching my stomach, making me feel sick. She was seventeen. Her whole life she'd lived under an assumption that I knew was false. It was time to tell her the truth. But it terrified me. Chilled me to the bone. What if she rejected me? The most important person in my world. Was it actually worth the risk of losing her just to tell her the truth? I could continue the deception. Keep going as I was. But I was single again and I was lying to myself, living a half-life, under the shadow of illusion. So, I decided to tell her the truth. And then I stalled. Weeks went by. Months went by. Until the discomfort of dishonesty compelled me to act. Every day while we were away, I planned to tell her, and then I found an excuse. Eventually, the day came when I knew it was the day. My mouth dry, the words rehearsed, I said that there was something I wanted to tell her, that might be nothing, but I wanted her to know. I shared that she might have the assumption I was straight. After all, I'd been married, and then engaged to another man. But in fact, I was bisexual. And even if I never date a woman again, I'll always be bi, and I wanted her to know. To see the full me. The real me. I held my breath. In fact, I think it just stopped; it wasn't even a conscious act. 'Well, I'm not surprised really,' she said. And that was the full conversation. Months of avoiding. Weeks of planning. Sleepless nights. Anxiety and fear. But finding my courage to sit down and have that conversation on a bed in New York released it all. Fully me, living with my daughter and letting myself be seen.

For the next seven days, I'd like you to notice the fear that comes up in your life. Make a list of all the things that you're scared about, where fear is getting in the way. You might discover that you put off having challenging conversations because you're scared of how the other person might react. Perhaps you'll realise that you avoid taking action in your life for fear of the consequences or being judged by other people. You maybe don't say how you actually feel in case the other person rejects you. Once you have made a list over a seven-day period, stop and take a look at what's on your list. Then for each thing, ask yourself the following questions: what if the story that I'm telling myself is just made up? What if the outcome was different and potentially more positive? I'm sure you'll find that you feel less stuck and inhibited. We all make up stories all the time about what will and won't happen. And most of the time, we then act as if those stories are real, regardless of the facts. As a friend of mine once said, 'If you're going to make up stories, at least make up good ones!' So now I'd like you to look at your list for a third time, and this time ask yourself different questions: what's the best thing that could possibly happen? Could it be that the step is worth taking after all?

Summary

I truly believe that these skills should be taught in schools. And since they haven't been yet, it's time for us all to start practising them. You won't build them all overnight, so pick the one that feels the most useful for you right now and start to put it into practice in the context of the current change you're facing. As with most things in this book, if you notice yourself feeling resistant towards any of the specific change skills, get curious about that. It could be that it offers you the greatest gift if you move towards it, and see what you discover about yourself.

You've now got the basics for:

- Finding your purpose
- Honouring your values
- Practising self-care
- Living with self-compassion
- Becoming friends with vulnerability
- Discovering your courage

Pause for just a minute or two and reflect on what becomes possible now that you have these things at your fingertips. It's quite a magical thought!

Notes

Chapter 10:
Using Change Tools

Introduction

This chapter sits alongside the change skills from the previous chapter, and there's a lot in it. It gives you all the tools you need to successfully live through change. Imagine if you were in the kitchen and cooking a tasty dinner. I've given you the recipe and the ingredients. This section gives the tools and techniques. So, if you didn't know how to melt butter and mix in flour to start off a white sauce before you add the milk, this is the place you would come for the instructions. It's here for you to dip into throughout your experience of change. In the preceding chapters, I've signposted some of these tools. You might want to read this section from start to finish so you know what's here. or just dip into it whenever seems relevant. If you're a parent, you might also find some of these tools useful for your kids. Children are constantly living through change, and it can sometimes feel overwhelming for them. These tools can help give them more control, which can help to reduce some of the behaviours we see when they don't feel like they have autonomy. If you're a leader or manager, these tools can help your teams. Many of them are core coaching tools, so if you've ever worked with a trained coach, some of them will seem familiar. In all the work I do with executive

> We are capable of creating almost anything we desire

leaders, these are the tools I use every single day. It's a total privilege to have tools that can help people with significant responsibilities to take action and create the changes that they want to create in their lives and organisations. Even after 25 years of working in change, it still surprises me sometimes how the simplest of interventions can create such seismic shifts. So, these tools come with a caution – they may change your life, but only if you want them to!

When you want to...	Use these tools
Get clear on what matters to you	Vision board
Unlock your thinking	Powerful questions
Discover what's holding you back	Gremlins
Do what you can't do alone	Ask for help
Get moving or stop being stuck	Accountability
Counteract negativity	Gratitude
Get into the present moment	Mindfulness
Recognise what's here for you now	Feelings and needs
Stop running around	Slow down

Making the vision tangible – creating a vision board

Our brains are incredibly powerful tools, and they are also pretty simple. We are capable of creating almost anything we desire – if we can dream it, we can create it. And while you might not personally believe that, you just need to look around you for evidence that this is true of humanity. Every single thing you can see in your current environment was once imagined by another human being. And you are just as capable of creating something. It helps to paint a picture of what we want to create. When we are setting out at the start of any path of change, whether we want to move house, start a family or change careers, or we just want to change our eating habits or get more intentional about how we spend our time. Even when we are facing change that is not of our choosing, it can help us to feel more empowered and less out of control if we can set some parameters for how we want to feel and experience this change. When I work with clients who are going through change that life has thrown at them, it's critical that we work together to put them back in the driving seat and have them set out the thoughts and ideas they have about what lies ahead.

The most powerful tool I know of, to help you communicate with your own brain about the change you want to create, is to make a vision board. Why? Because it is so tangible and will sit on your desk or wall while you face change day in and day out. And because, if you truly settle in while you create it, you do tap into your unconscious mind and access the things that genuinely matter to you. It's a creative process for anyone who can use a pair of scissors and a glue stick. I've sat with clients as they've cut things out of magazines and stuck them on to a piece of paper. Months, even years, later, those things become a reality and the client can see the power of creating that visual.

Like all of my tools, this can be done in fifteen-minute sections, though we do need two of them to create a vision board. In the first fifteen minutes, you'll gather together images, and then in the second fifteen minutes, you'll put those images together.

Step 1: Gather images

You will need: a pile of magazines, newspapers, catalogues or anything that you don't mind cutting up into pieces!

You can choose to go old school or twenty-first century for this process. I prefer old school, cutting and sticking and making it messy rather than perfectly straight lines. And some people prefer to go digital. You could always try both and see which you prefer. If you're going to go with the digital version, you'll follow the same process, just instead of ripping images and words from magazines etc, you'll find them online in either free image libraries or Pinterest. It can be helpful if you're doing that to look for broad search terms and to think a little offbeat in what you type into the search bar. So, if you have a theme of joy, you might search for the word 'joy' and also then search for 'happy', 'fulfilled', 'play' or 'delight' as well as any other words that are connected in your mind. The way you define joy will be different from other people, so give yourself as much random search material as possible.

Start by setting an intention or a time frame for the vision board. You might want to create it for what you want in the next year (I always create a vision board at the start of each year) or for a particular change e.g. a new job or career or even a relationship. Take a few minutes to sit quietly (or as quietly as you can if you have other people or pets around!) and just take some slow breaths to shut out the day-to-day hustle and bustle and chatter in your head. Once you feel settled, say what it is that you are creating this vision board for, ideally out loud, but in your head will do if that's all that's possible. In recent years, I've created vision boards for my overall life for the next three to five years, for the specific theme I've chosen for each year and also for the creation of a new home. Each one has been completely different and sometimes I haven't had a clue what some of the things meant, but they felt important to include.

Now you're going to take fifteen minutes – set a timer – to go through magazines or newspapers etc and pull out images that seem to speak to you. Not literally, of course, but images that make you think, *ah* or *yes*, or that you just want to include. You might actually end up ditching some of them and that's perfectly okay, just make a pile of possible images for your theme. Some might surprise you and seem to make no sense at all – that's also okay. And some might thrill you or give you a feeling of edge or challenge; let them all join the pile. Even if you are normally a neat and tidy person, please try to just go with the flow in this process. Rip out the pages rather than cutting neatly around particular words or images – we want it all to be a bit messy at this stage. Notice if you feel inclined to keep going once the timer tells you time's up! The reason we set a timer is because it makes it feel manageable and achievable. It's so easy to tell ourselves that these are big activities and not do them. My first ever coach was the person who encouraged me to get my first vision board created back in 2008 because she told me to set a timer and give myself a maximum of twenty minutes to get the images together and ten minutes to stick them all down. It was the only thing that made it feel achievable, so set the timer and stick to it. If you want to keep going, you can always create another vision board for another aspect of your life!

Step 2: Put them together

You will need: a bigger piece of paper (A3 or ledger paper), a glue stick and maybe some scissors (if you're doing a digital version you can use Canva or other collage apps, or you can print out your images and then go old school for this second stage).

Now's the fun part, and it's important that you set a timer

and stick to it, or those perfectionism tendencies will try and stop you in your tracks. You're going to put the images together on the page. You might find you want to group things in a particular way, or to have lots of white space, or none at all. Trust your instinct and try not to overthink it. Go with what feels right and try not to judge yourself as you go. This is one other reason for using a timer. If you have to keep going at pace, you have less time to stop and question what you're doing. The main thing is to get all your images and words on to the page. They might overlap, they might not, and that doesn't matter.

If, as you're sticking things down, you find something that you just don't want on the page, that's okay. Think of this as final editorial control. You get to choose what makes the final cut. What I do tend to do with those things is to keep them for a few days and just check back with myself in a week or so and see if they maybe do belong on the vision board after all, and then I stick them on. Sometimes my subconscious has me pull an image or word out of a magazine in step 1, and then in step 2, my conscious mind overrules the decision, and it doesn't make the cut. After a few days, something seems to shift and my subconscious convinces my conscious mind to include it after all. Try it and see what shows up.

Congratulations! You've made your vision board and can now find somewhere to put it where you will see it regularly and it can inspire you throughout your change. I tend to take a photo of my vision board and have it on my phone as my wallpaper and sometimes print it out and put a smaller version in my planner or journal, so that I have easy access to it. I'm sure your vision board will inspire and motivate you and help you thrive through change!

The power of questions and enquiry to access your own wisdom

Did you know you are way more clever and insightful than you realise? In fact, the chances are you probably have the answers for how to create or live through change in your life within you. So often, we don't actually believe that we are completely resourceful and have what we need. And yet, when we take the time and the space to access our own innate wisdom, we can astonish ourselves at what we know and are capable of. The easiest way to access our own inner knowing is to simply ask and listen. When I work with new coaches as a coach supervisor, they often tangle themselves in knots trying to find the 'best' question or the 'right' question to ask a coaching client. They are caught up in the belief that there is, somewhere out there, a magical question that will unlock everything for their client and justify their hourly rate. In fact, it often surprises them to know that there is no such question.

Similarly, it can surprise coaching clients when they ask me, 'What do you mean by that question?' and I say, 'I don't know!' The reality is, in coaching, we are asking questions as doorways, and we never know what's on the other side. The door might be locked; it might be sticky; there might be a nightmare on the other side or

> When we take the time and the space to access our own innate wisdom, we can astonish ourselves

something truly magical. Only when we ask the questions do we open up the possibility to discover what's on the other side. And so it is with asking yourself something – you create the potential for new wisdom to be revealed, just by asking the question. The even better thing is that this new-found wisdom is free and available to you at any time, day or night, because you are always there to ask and to listen to the answer.

Let's try it now. Ask yourself, 'what do I need to know right now?', and then sit quietly and listen. Just notice what you're aware of. You might think you hear an answer or become aware of something that you weren't previously. If you pay attention and just keep breathing, something will likely occur to you that you hadn't been thinking before. That inner voice wants you to pay more attention. If you're facing change of any sort, then being able to access it whenever you choose to is going to give you more to work with.

The even better news is that we can turbo-charge that inner wisdom when we write down the answers for ourselves. This is the basic premise of journalling, writing for the sake of our own insight and deeper understanding. You can choose to write down a question and then write down the answers, and see what comes up. Here are some questions to get you started:

- What do I need to know now?
- What's in my best interest today?
- What's getting in my way?
- What's the greatest gift I have just now?
- How am I sabotaging myself?
- How can I be my greatest support?
- Who am I today?
- Where can I get support today?
- What's the next step for me to take?
- What can I do to take care of myself?

You'll notice that all of these questions are short and open-ended. And you might also have noticed that there are no questions that start with 'why'. As anyone who's ever been near a toddler will know, questions that start with 'why' tend to drive you crazy. They also prompt you to defend yourself in the answer – it almost feels like the question is attacking you. If you want to get to the root cause of something, you can ask things like, 'what's important about that?' or 'what else?' or even, 'what's the most important piece?' rather than asking 'why...?'.

If you're working through some significant change and you want to use that to help you understand more about yourself, you can ask more enquiry-like questions. These tend to be questions that will make you stop and think, rather than the ones that you can answer straight away. The kinds of questions that invite you to pause and reflect and write pages in response rather than a few lines. Being able to ask yourself enquiries will also help to deepen your self-awareness and give even more fuel for your future. Here are some enquiries to get you started, and I'm sure you'll have plenty of other ideas:

- What's my future?
- Who am I becoming?
- What's the role of this change in my life?
- Where am I holding back?
- What do I truly long for?
- What's the core of this change?
- How can I use this to help me?
- What's the growth here?
- What can I let go?
- What's next?

By taking the time to reflect and get curious about your own thinking and sense-making, you will always uncover more. Even asking yourself the same question on different days will enable you to discover different aspects of yourself that can support you, as you learn to thrive through change. Give yourself access to the wisdom within you by picking up pen and paper now and seeing what emerges. And in case you're worried about getting it wrong, you can't. Whatever flows from your pen is relevant, even when it feels like it's not. Let the words fall on to the paper. Try not to judge them and see what emerges.

If you'd like more space for your thoughts to become untangled, you can use the companion journal for Untangled available through all good bookshops.

Getting to know your gremlins or inner allies

I was born in 1977. The *Gremlins* film came out when I was just at the right age to be terrified by those evil ones and captivated by Gizmo. That's not the kind of gremlins I'm talking about here. In fact, you may choose not to see them as gremlins but to see them as allies. I'm talking about the different parts of you and the different aspects of yourself, or the variety of things you say to yourself in your own head. When I first completed my coach training, I was introduced to this as gremlins, or saboteurs, which is why I've called this section what I have. Since then, I've learned more ways of thinking about yourself, and I actually believe that it's more helpful to look at our internal dialogue as different aspects of ourselves that are trying to keep us safe.

In practical terms, I'm talking about the voices in your mind that stop you from engaging with change. The self-criticism or self-judgement. The voice that says *you'll be too big for your own good if you do X, Y or Z.* The constant inner chatter that says, *don't bother to do A, B or C because you'll never succeed anyway or people will judge you for it*. The thoughts that keep you awake at night saying, *you're not doing enough*, or *you're doing too much*. The voices in our head that are rarely satisfied.

Through decades of helping people through change, I can tell you that you are not the only one who has that going on in your mind. Everyone does. What we do with the chatter, how much we listen to it and what influence it has on our life, varies. And you can learn how to handle it, but you can't make it go away. Because, ultimately, those voices are all on the same side. They all want to keep you safe and protect you from being hurt. They might sometimes have interesting ideas about what's likely to happen if you step into change. Often, they think that the way things are is the safest for you, psychologically speaking. And they usually don't like things that rock the boat. So, they can be very persuasive and convince you that doing nothing is the best plan. They can prevent you from applying for jobs. They can tell you to stay in relationships rather than have the challenging conversations to change things. I've even seen them stopping clients from trying new hobbies or moving house. A good friend of mine talks about the 'shitty committee' – she reckons she has several different members, but they're all out to hold her back from moving forward with her life.

So, what do we do about them? I used to take quite a combative approach to this, but I've softened a little as I've learned more about the psychology and the vital role that these gremlins play in our lives. So now, I'm going to invite you to notice the thoughts that you have every day (it's the reason we do so much journalling). Then start to look at those thoughts and ask yourself where they come from. Are they helping you to move forward? Or are they more fear-based? Do they come from the grounded, centred, level-headed version of yourself, or do they come from a place of anxiety and protection? If they come from a place of fear and protection, it might be time to look at how real that fear is and what you actually want and need. One of my therapists once asked me, 'If the fear wasn't there, what would you do?' I still come back to that question. If I could strip out the fear, what do I want?

So, one tool to have in your back pocket as you live through change is the ability to separate out the different thoughts and feelings in your mind and choose what to do with them. Do they get to run the show, or do you just acknowledge the thought and say quietly to yourself, *'Thank you, I know you're trying to keep me safe, and I can handle this.'*

Asking for help – it's not a four-letter word

I'm going to be honest and say I should probably have started the whole book with this particular tool, because it truly is a vital part of helping yourself to thrive through change. Particularly if you are busy, juggling multiple responsibilities, and either trying to create change of your choosing or cope with the kind life throws your way.

For some reason, human beings have an inherent flaw in our development. We spend years helping our kids to become independent and to learn to do things themselves rather than have to ask others for help. This then backfires when we reach adulthood, and we would actually benefit from asking for help, but we don't because we think we are meant to go it alone. I remember when my daughter was only around three years old, and she was going through a big developmental leap. She was convinced that she could be entirely independent. I bought her a kids' book that I saw called *I can do anything that's everything, all by myself*, because it just seemed so entirely apt. Whatever it was that she faced from day to day, she could do it 'all by myself'. No matter if she wasn't actually tall enough, or it involved a hot pan, she was determined to try and do it all solo. And the truth is, most of us keep that stubborn determination way into our adult lives, if not forever. We carry on, struggling or overstretching ourselves, resolute in our commitment to do it ourselves. And in facing change, that can be the thing that either stops us from getting the outcome we had envisaged or makes the route to get there way harder than it needs to be.

And I will admit at this point that I get it. I was a card-carrying member of the 'I can do anything that's everything, all by myself' club. When I was growing up, independence was rewarded and recognised as being a highly desirable attribute. And for good reason. It's generally pretty frowned upon to rely on others for everything. But I was, perhaps, too good a student for this particular lesson, and I went all out to be completely independent, to rely on no-one, no matter what the cost. It's not a clever strategy. I was the woman struggling to carry all the groceries, whilst insisting that I was fine. More importantly, I was the woman struggling with my life, while refusing all offers of help. And I definitely wasn't going to ask for it. The stories I made up about what it meant to ask for help were horrific. I should add that those stories only applied to me, of course. Anyone else asking for help was smart, and I was more than happy to help them.

Then one day, many years ago, something changed. I reached a point when I was out of all other options. I had hit some bumps in the road with my business, and my cash was flowing all the wrong way. I felt like I had no other option and, finally, in an act of desperation, I sent an email to key people I trusted and asked them for help to try and raise a small amount of investment. I hit 'send' on the email, and I ran and locked myself in my bathroom. I felt terrified of the judgement and condemnation that I was sure would be the response, even though these were people I trusted and who I thought supported me. I needed to hide. To not be seen. I was convinced I was a failure. In my mind, they were going to respond and accuse me of being a terrible businesswoman who should have known better and who had no chance if I couldn't fix this problem myself. In fact, I had probably just sealed the fate for the ending of my business.

Eventually, I realised I couldn't actually stay in my bathroom forever and, some considerable time later, I ventured out to the rest of my apartment. By the time I got back to the kitchen where my iPad still sat open, I already had two texts on my phone from people I had emailed. Both of them offered support, saying they'd meet with me to get some plans together, and they were glad I'd asked for help. It's no exaggeration to say that I literally crumpled on the floor in floods of tears. Not only because there now seemed to be a future for my business – which I started and continue because I love the work and it had looked like it was coming to an end – but also because they hadn't condemned me for asking for help, as I thought they would. The business ultimately secured a small level of investment at that stage and is now more than twelve years old and thriving. Asking for help isn't a bad thing. It's a good thing. You might not believe me. I understand that.

On that day I learned, truly learned, that it's not only okay to ask for help, but it's actually important to do so. If I hadn't got out of my own way and asked for help, the business would have collapsed. Not only would I have had to find something else to do, but so would my team, and our clients would have had to access different solutions. The ripple effect could have been significant. Instead, the ripple effect of my asking for help was, and continues to be, significant. In learning that lesson, I am now much more readily able to ask for help for the small stuff as well as the big. Sometimes we need to learn the lessons in big ways to give us access to them day to day.

In terms of the change that you're currently facing, you may feel like your need for help is small or large, the barrier to accessing it tiny or massive. Whatever the case, I want you to now write down the answers to the following:

- What help do you need?
- Who might be able to help you?

And now, putting your concerns over here, where I can hold them for you for a while, I want you to reach out to that person or those people and ask them to help you. I mean now – I'll wait. Pick up the phone and call them, or send them the email or text. Ask them now to help you and simply see what happens next. My biggest tip for this is to keep breathing, and the next one is to keep your request for help as general as you can. You might be surprised what shows up.

The chances are, the person is willing and able to help you and their help could actually exceed your wildest dreams. And on the off-chance that they aren't able to help you for some reason or another, you can ask them who they know who *can* help you. Simply stay in the belief that there is help available and that it's not only okay to ask for it, it's a vital part of being an adult. This will keep you on the right path. You are no longer the kid or teenager developing and demonstrating your independence. You're an adult who has the absolute benefit of being able to ask others to help you and then actually let them do so. Because, of course, you do actually need to let people help, and that in itself can be challenging. But for today, we're focusing on asking for help. So, if you've been stalling, now is the time to pick up the phone and ask for the help you need. You can do this. I completely believe in you. Reach out and let that person help you. And see what happens next.

Here are some examples of the kinds of help you might ask for (because if you're ultra-independent it can be hard to even think about what others might be able to help you with):

- Looking after your kids or pets for a bit because there is something you want to do (not just something you have to do).
- Helping you research something to do with your chosen change, e.g. potential estate agents to sell your house.
- Baking you a cake because you need cheering up.
- Spending an evening with you sorting out old photographs for a funeral you need to arrange.
- Staying on the phone with you while you fall asleep because you don't want to be alone (I have actually done this for a friend).
- Sitting with you while you phone the doctor to make the appointment you don't want to make.
- Going shopping with you for clothes for a job interview.
- Reviewing your business plans even when they are really sketchy, and you don't want anyone else to see them.
- Working with you to set out your monthly budget or your current financial position even when you are resisting it to the hilt.
- Getting out for a walk with you because you know you need to start to exercise and it just all feels too hard.

The biggest example I have ever had of the power of accepting help was many, many years ago. But I'll never forget it. It was a late October evening, and I had stayed late at work with a colleague. Realising how late it was, she rushed off to catch her train home and left me to finish up our notes. Rumour had it that the office building was supposed to be haunted - I decided not to stick around and find out!

Walking towards the centre of the city, I decided to go to the bookshop to kill some time. My train was over an hour's wait. Better to wait somewhere warm. Plus, I can never refuse time in a bookshop. In the semi-darkness, I saw a young woman ahead of me, sitting by the side of the road, in the cold and the dark. A stranger in front of me glanced at her and muttered the words, 'You alright?' with barely a passing glance.

'Yeah,' she replied with equally little conviction. I kept walking. A few steps further. And as I did, I slowed a little. Was she alright? Really? She didn't look it. Her face was tear-stained. She was sitting in the dark on her own. It was late October, in Scotland. I turned back and walked towards her.

'Are you really okay?' I asked, crouching down beside her.

'No,' she responded, this time the truth. 'I've done something stupid... I've taken too many pills'. The chill wrapped around my body. Fear gripped me as I tried to grapple with what to say next, how to reach out to her, what would help us to connect.

'Do you want me to help you?' I asked, holding my breath for the answer, knowing that how she replied would determine what happened from here.

'Yes,' came her voice, barely audible.

'*Okay*,' was my response, more powerful now, certain that she had given me the permission I needed to take the steps from here.

Several hours later as we sat in the emergency department, I learned more about her story, but more importantly I learned more about her, her brilliance, her magic, her sparkle. She had just turned eighteen, fallen through the cracks of the mental health care service and was on the edge of life. But she wanted help. She accepted my offer of help. It literally saved her life that night. Years later, she messaged me to say thank you. I'd left my number in her bag, so that she knew she was never alone again. She thinks I was her guardian angel that night. I think she asked for help, and I responded. Help is not a four-letter word. It can be the thing that stops you from falling off the edge of the earth. Where is it time for you to say 'yes' to an offer of help?

Accountability to bust your own BS

I hate to break it to you, but there will be parts of any change – even change you long for – that you just don't want to do. And you can try to sweeten that with telling yourself that it's part of something bigger, which will help to some extent. But, ultimately, there will still be times when you're staring right at something you need to do and you just don't want to. Or maybe you want to, but you're scared to, or think you can't do it, or just want to be on the other side of it. This is where accountability comes in. The act of sharing what you're going to do with another human so that they can hold you to it. And yes, you can hold yourself accountable, but there are times when you just need to commit to your intention and get someone else to hold you to it. Let me be completely clear though: this is not about giving someone else permission to criticise you if you fall short. There can be no judgement involved in this – otherwise all you do is build the fear and self-criticism. What I'm talking about is compassionate accountability, the deal you make with a friend or someone close whom you trust, that

> Help is not a four-letter word. It can be the thing that stops you from falling off the edge of the earth

you are going to do the thing, on a certain day, maybe even at a certain time, and then you are going to let them know once you've done it. You are building in a backup plan for yourself so that when you want to wriggle out of it – and you will try – you know that there is somebody else expecting you to follow through and not back out.

In coaching when we hold accountability for clients, we ask three things:

- What will you do?
- By when?
- How will I know?

And sometimes we ask a bonus question:

- How do you want me to be with you, if you don't follow through?

These four questions give you a framework to design with your friend what will work best for you. Without the fourth question, there is a risk that you avoid them if you decide you can't actually do the thing you said you would. You need to know that your friend is not going to come down hard on you, that their response will be what you need from them. Maybe you need them to remind you of what was important about the thing in the first place. Perhaps you need them to say they'll sit with you while you take the step. Or to redesign an interim, baby step that you can take before you go for the bigger leap. Design with them what you need, and you're building yourself more scaffolding to help you take action and follow through.

Even in writing this book I have had to create accountability at every step of the way. Otherwise, I simply would not have got it written. Without the accountability I built in for myself, my fear would have always continued to run the show. The accountability needed to be stronger than the fear. The support available greater than the threat that I perceived.

The power of having someone else on your side, holding the support rope while you climb to new heights, is indescribable. Let someone else be there for you, and I guarantee you'll achieve more than you ever imagined.

Gratitude – the antidote to guilt

The practice of gratitude has gained in popularity over recent years, but I want to help you to understand how it can help you with living through change. Specifically, I want to show how gratitude can be the antidote to guilt we often feel, the sense that we've done something bad. Note that guilt is different from shame, the sense that we are bad. With guilt, the focus is on the behaviour, whereas with shame, the focus is on the person.

As an entrepreneur, single mum and someone who's always been committed to my own learning and development, I have been riddled with guilt for longer than I can remember. There is always a ready-to-find list of things that I feel guilty for – from not making a nutritious enough dinner for my daughter and me, to forgetting to get the thing that my daughter has asked me to get; from being late for picking her up from school because a meeting ran over, to leaving a meeting before it finished to ensure that I wouldn't be late to pick her up. The guilt, at times, has felt never-ending. My heart races. I feel a bit queasy. And somehow when we are facing change – whether it's of our choosing or not – the guilt levels rise. When I'm choosing to create

> When we are facing change – whether it's of our choosing or not – the guilt levels rise

change in my life, I feel guilty that I'm prioritising myself and my dreams or desires. However, when I'm responding to change that has fallen across my path, like a branch of a tree after a storm, I feel guilty that I'm being dragged away from my core priority. I resent having to shoehorn in time to respond to change and the demands that makes on my time. I don't like it. The feeling that I'm not doing the right thing. Or the sense that I'm doing the wrong thing. When I crawl into bed at night and my mind starts to list all the things that I haven't done, it can seem never-ending. And in some ways, it is.

Gratitude can be your salvation if you are also afflicted by guilt. The simple act of stopping and paying attention to what we're grateful for, creates a shift in our mindset that somehow eases the guilt and reorientates us to a calmer state.

Different people practise gratitude differently, but here are three ways that you can try to start to build a gratitude practice that works for you. As with each of these tools, the more you use them, the more you know you can reach for them whenever you need them most. A bit like if you only use a certain gadget in your kitchen or garden once every so often, you might need to read the instructions each time you get them out. With gratitude and other practices, if you literally do practise, regularly, at least for an initial period like thirty days, you build your own awareness of what works for you. This makes it easier to return to when you do truly need it.

And when you notice yourself feeling guilty about something, start to look for what it is that you can be grateful for; slowly, you'll start to rewire your thinking. For example, when I feel guilty that I'm late for picking my daughter up, I start to feel grateful that I have a daughter. I take a minute to be thankful that I'm able to pick her up from school, that she and I are safe and well, and that

I have a job that gives me meaningful and fulfilling conversations. I'm sure you can sense the difference that this thinking brings me on a Tuesday afternoon as I sit stuck at traffic lights watching the minutes tick by!

Gratitude journalling

Keeping a gratitude journal where you write down things you're grateful for can be a simple way to start to pay attention. You might want to set yourself a specific number of things to write down every day; you might want to write a short list, or longer explanations of what made you grateful. For me it has to be simple and short, or I lose the practice. So, I've done lists of three things I'm grateful for on my phone in the notes app last thing at night, or I've had a small journal next to my bed and written down five things that I was grateful for right before I turn out the light. Whatever works for you to make it a practice that you can stick to is the most important thing. I also like to look back over the things that I've listed and notice any patterns. For example, one year I kept a physical gratitude journal for pretty much the whole year, and I noticed that there were definitely things that kept coming up over and over again. With that awareness, I was able to intentionally choose to do more of those things in my life.

Gratitude jar

This can be a fun approach to try if you'd like to involve others in your household. We did this one year and it was great to look back at the end of the year and see what things we had already forgotten about. You'll need a bowl or a box – we used a glass goldfish-style bowl, pens and paper or sticky notes or something that you can write on regularly. Every time you think of something to be grateful for, you write a note on a piece of paper or a folded sticky note (so they don't get stuck together!) and pop it into the jar. You can also put actual objects in the jar. Our jar ended up with a cork from a bottle of Prosecco to celebrate an event, a funny decoration from an ice-cream sundae that we had as a shared treat one day and a small Christmas decoration that we both loved. The benefit of using a jar is that it is a visual reminder to think of things that you're grateful for, so keep it somewhere prominent so that you will remember to add to it. You can, of course, make it a daily or weekly practice to sit down and intentionally add to the jar or you can make it more sporadic when things occur to you.

Gratitude photos

For those of you who are more visual, you might want to take a photograph each day of something you're grateful for. This is one I tried in 2022 and I created a specific folder for them on Instagram, so that I could look back and see them over time. Taking only one image a day means you have to focus on what you're truly grateful for, and, of course, some things aren't easy to put into image, but it is a different creative way to capture what you notice other than using words.

Gratitude walk

Lastly, you can start a habit of going for a gratitude walk – even around your house. This one comes from Jack Canfield, and he recommends you simply walk around and say what you are grateful for. For example; 'I'm grateful for the electricity that heats my home. I'm grateful for my family whose laughter fills the living room. I'm grateful for the people who made the chair I sit on. I'm grateful for the scent of the candle that helps me relax. I'm grateful for...' Jack says that this act raises your energetic vibration and, quite simply, it makes you feel better. We all find it so easy to take things for granted and the act of practising gratitude does reorientate that. And if you are feeling guilty about not having done the dishes, you can simply express your gratitude that you have dishes to do, hot water and detergent to do them with and music to listen to while you do them!

Breathing and the dreaded 'M' word (mindfulness)

I talked about mindfulness previously as one element of self-compassion, because it's a core part of that skill. I wanted to include it again here, firstly because it's something I've struggled with, and I know I'm not alone in that, and secondly, I wanted to give you a more tools-oriented view.

In the context of change, being more mindful helps you to remove the chatter in your head, not by making it go away, but more by making you focus on it less. And before I share any techniques, let me remind you of my biggest learning here: mindfulness is a practice. It's not something that you can get right or wrong; there is no performance; it's just a constant commitment to coming back to yourself, over and over and over again. So, there is no way you can get this wrong. There is no way to fail. You just practise and, like a toddler learning to walk, you don't even realise when you're doing it – it just happens.

> Mindfulness is a practice. It's not something that you can get right or wrong; there is no performance

A quick search on Google will show you that there are literally millions of places you can find out more about mindfulness. It can seem like a complete jungle and, if you get caught up in wanting to do it 'right', that jungle can seem formidable. Which is why my biggest tip is: just start. Whatever you do, spend a couple of minutes today, sixty seconds if that's all you can cope with, practising mindfulness. And then tomorrow, do the same again.

And the day after, perhaps you'll manage an extra ten seconds. Then maybe the day after you'll go back a step and manage sixty seconds again. It doesn't matter. The key is that you are practising mindfulness – that's what does matter.

Here are four techniques you can try to get started, and remember you will find something that feels more like it's right for you – just keep experimenting. You might find you prefer listening to someone in a guided meditation. Or you might hate that and feel much more comfortable just getting outside and doing a mindful walk. Whatever your practice, if it's helping you to connect with yourself and become more aware of what's going on for you, keep going!

Mindful breathing

For this approach, you're going to focus on your breathing. Start by sitting comfortably, with your back in an upright position (though I have been known to practise mindfulness when I'm still in bed and lying down, so do whatever works for you!). Feel your feet on the floor and your body where it makes contact with the chair or cushion. Without changing your breath, start to become aware of it. Notice where the breath enters your body. Perhaps you might be aware of the cold as it enters your nostrils or the way your chest rises as your lungs fill. Just pay attention to where you feel your breath, as you breathe in and as you breathe out. Any time you notice your thoughts or become aware of thinking or feeling, bring your attention back to the breath and notice where it is in your body.

Progressive body relaxation

This is a technique I used to use a lot with my daughter when she was around eleven years old and struggled to fall asleep. Lying down, you are going to start with your feet and slowly work your way up the whole length of your body, feeling each muscle and part of your body relax in turn. So, starting with your toes, feel your toes soften and relax, heavy and sinking into the bed. Now feel the soles of your feet as they sink into the bed, heavy, soft and relaxed. Then feel your ankles soften and relax, heavy and sinking into the bed. Work your way up your whole body, until you reach your face and your head, heavy, soft and relaxed. You might find it helpful to play a progressive body relaxation recording to follow the voice along in your own mind.

Counting breaths

The third technique is similar to the first one in that you are going to focus on your breath. This time, however, you're going to count your breaths. As before, start by getting comfortable in your chair in an upright position. Let any outside distractions fall away as you start to pay attention to your breath. Breathing in slowly and then breathing out slowly, count to one. Breathing in slowly and then breathing out slowly, count to two. Keep breathing in and out, with a count for each complete breath cycle until you reach a count of ten. If you would like to practise for longer, you can start again from one. If you get distracted by your own thoughts, simply return to the breath and resume counting from when you last remember.

Tracing your hand

For this final technique, you're going to use the index finger of your right hand (we'll call this your working hand) to trace the outline of your left hand (we'll call this your static hand). Start by holding your static hand palm towards you and put the index finger of your working hand at the base of your smallest finger. As you run the index finger up that smallest finger, breathe in and as you then trace the index finger down the smallest finger, breathe out. Run the index finger of the working hand up the ring finger of the static hand, breathing in, and then run the index finger down the ring finger, breathing out. Keep tracing the outline of your hand with that index finger, breathing in on the way up and breathing out on the way down. You can then swap hands and use the index finger on your left hand to trace the outline of your right hand, repeating the breathing pattern, in on the way up, out on the way down.

You might discover that you prefer some of these techniques to others. You'll find many, many more online. Start with experimenting with something, and remember that the point of doing this is both to increase your self-compassion and to reduce the impact of the unhelpful chatter in your mind as you live through change.

Feelings and needs

Change brings a lot of feelings with it, and if we don't pay attention to those feelings, they can end up running the show, through our behaviours. Typically, when I'm facing any kind of change in my life, there will be points when I feel overwhelmed, anxious, excited, creative or even just uncertain. I can choose to ignore those feelings, or to not even notice them, and when I do, I usually get bitten in the ass. Because our feelings are like signposts, giving us information about what we're experiencing. And if I'm feeling excited, that might be a signpost to keep going. Whereas if I'm feeling overwhelmed, it might mean it's time to pause and take stock. Of course, the reverse might also be true – overwhelm might mean keep going; excitement might mean pause. Because there is no universal or linear mapping of feelings to needs. But by starting to become more aware of how we feel and asking ourselves what we need, the chances of unproductive behaviour running the show reduces. Sometimes just the act of noticing how we feel or sharing it with someone is in fact enough for it to move on. You can even try it now. How are you feeling right now? As I sit here writing, I'm actually feeling a bit apprehensive. The sunlight is starting to fade, and I wanted to get this section finished and get out for a short walk before it starts to get too dark. I notice that I'm feeling edgy because I'm not sure that I have enough time for both. How are you feeling? Really feeling? Maybe even write down one or two words in the margin right now. It's perfectly possible to feel more than one feeling at a time. Even when I'm facing small change, like starting a new habit, I can feel a mixture of motivated and a bit apprehensive or concerned.

Once you know how you feel, you can also start to identify what you need. And sometimes that might be something, or sometimes it might actually be nothing. It just helps to ask yourself the question. This can also be incredibly useful with children, particularly when they are overwrought or can't express how they feel. You can even use pictures of different faces showing different emotions and have them choose which one is closest to how they feel.

Let's practise now. Stick with the feeling you identified earlier, and ask yourself: what do I need? So, in my example of the sunlight fading as I raced to get this section written, when I ask myself that question, I realise I need to trust that there is enough time for both the writing and the walk, and I also need to notice the time because it is in fact ages until the sun sets – it just feels later than it is! You might find that when you ask yourself what you need, you get the answer 'I don't know'. Sometimes we're just not used to asking ourselves and listening to the answer. At times we feel so completely overwhelmed or triggered that we can't seem to access the part of our brain that has the ability to think through what we need. If that's the case, just notice that and revisit how you're feeling. It's okay to not know. And it's also okay to take the time to just feel what you're feeling. The main thing is that you're starting to build the muscle of noticing how you feel and asking yourself what you need. If you think about it, sometimes we go into a restaurant for dinner and we don't know what we want to eat – this is not a new problem! Give yourself a little time. Like the waiter in the restaurant, you could even offer yourself some options or ask a few further questions to narrow down the options a little. For example, do you want space or company with others? Would a hug help or is it more useful to make a list of what's overwhelming you? You could even try to ask yourself, 'what if I did know?', because sometimes we do actually know and we just won't acknowledge it to ourselves. Simply asking the question can help us cut through our own self-filtering process.

As you live through change, noticing how you feel and what you need will help you stay alert and conscious of your own reactions and responses. It can also start to remove some of the roadblocks that might get in your way. If you start to notice yourself becoming overwhelmed, or doubting yourself, or even scared of failure, you can bring yourself back to your overall purpose and mission and enable yourself to keep moving.

Notice how you feel now as you finish reading this section. Maybe you feel the same as you did earlier; perhaps it's already changed. We are not our feelings, but they do influence us and, as Brené Brown says in *Dare to Lead*™, 'Leaders must either invest a reasonable amount of time attending to fears and feelings, or squander an unreasonable amount of time trying to manage ineffective and unproductive behaviour.' In my view, you can replace the word 'leaders' with 'we', because when we don't pay attention to our fears and our feelings, we end up being caught up in our behaviours. You now have the tools to start to pay attention to how you feel.

Slowing down to speed up

In the twenty-first century we live fast. Our daily lives are full of speed, momentum and energy. And when they are slower than we'd like them to be, we can often become frustrated and feel disempowered. But to thrive through change, we sometimes need to slow things down, to ease up on the relentless pursuit of forwards momentum and moderate the pace. When we relax a little and take the pressure off ourselves, we can find a deeper connection with what truly matters. We might get new insight, or increased clarity, or discover a hidden energy reserve which powers us through the next stage of our transformation. In that way, slowing down is almost a kind of mindfulness practice. As as you did in the earlier section, you might notice you have some resistance to even the idea of going slower than you usually do. For today, I want to invite you to experiment, simply try it out and see what happens. As I write this, I have just finished making myself a cup of coffee. At home I use the latest coffee machine; everything happens at the press of one button and it's pretty much instantaneous. Good coffee at my fingertips. Right now, I'm not at home – I'm tucked up in a studio on a hillside, where things seem to automatically go at a more natural pace. So, I made my coffee in a cafetière or French press. It's slower. I have to wait for the coffee grounds to infuse the water and then press the plunger down, rather than the hot water being shot under pressure through the coffee like it does in my machine. And somehow, there is more ritual involved. More gratitude for the cup of coffee that emerges from the process. I have increased awareness of what it takes to make a cup of coffee. And I'm not going to get evangelical about going backwards in time. There is absolutely a place for new inventions and developments that make our lives easier. Sometimes though, it can help to take things at a different pace. Just as a trial, I'd like you to test out what you notice when you slow down and let things expand a little. Here are two ways you can try today:

Experiment 1: Slow your walking pace

This experiment is so simple, and you can even do it in your house, though I would recommend getting outside, ideally into nature, if you can. You can also involve any children, although if they're little they'll find it almost as tricky as you might! Start off by walking for a minute or so at your usual walking pace. Just walk and see how you feel. Then I want you to slow your walking pace to half the speed and walk for another minute or so. Keep walking and see how you feel and what you notice. Next, slow your pace to half the speed again. Again, walk and see what arises in your awareness. Each time, slow your speed by half until you are conscious of each part of your foot as it leaves the ground. Notice the way your body moves forward and the individual muscles of your body help you to keep walking. If you're outside, you'll probably start to feel a bit daft and worry that people are looking at you, and that's okay – keep going with the practice or move somewhere with fewer people if that makes you feel more comfortable. Once you feel like you can't possibly go any slower, you can end the practice. Pay attention to how you feel, what your thoughts are and what you're aware of. You might want to journal about the experience so that you have notes to come back to.

Experiment 2: Slow your shower

When you next have a shower, I want you to slow each stage

down. Having a shower tends to be a pretty automatic thing for most people. We follow a set pattern; we do things on autopilot; and we shower as quickly and efficiently as possible – at least in the morning when we're getting ready for work. Today it's time to slow it down. Take time to let the water fall over your body. Let the steam fill your nostrils and breathe in deeply. Nourish your body as you wash yourself and notice the way the water feels on your skin. Slow it down and let yourself be fully present. As well as being a form of mindfulness, you might notice that the act of slowing down will prompt new awareness or new thoughts. You might feel more invigorated than you do after your regular shower.

Slowing down can actually bring us more speed

I've deliberately chosen two things that will be accessible to most people. And, of course, if you use a wheelchair or other mobility device, you can use the same approach to slow down your movement.

As you experiment with this process, you might actually start to feel more tired and in need of rest. I actually think that's why most of us stay busy and fast and avoid the reduction in pace. Arguably, you feel that way because you need to slow down and recharge your batteries. If that's what you're noticing, perhaps it's time to build more rest and recuperation into your calendar, for which you will probably need to say 'no' and adjust your own expectations of what you can achieve in twenty-four hours. Believe me, I know how hard that is, and it is worth it so that you can focus on what truly matters to you.

Slowing down can actually bring us more speed. We can re-energise ourselves, become more aware of what we truly want and need, and gain new insight and clarity to inform the change we face. Whilst these are two specific activities to give you a physical experience of slowing down, you can now bring the same approach to real parts of your life. What gift would it bring if you reduced the speed of things like the time frame to make a decision, or the deadline you set yourself to achieve a goal? One of my key mantras for goal setting is to set your goals in concrete but your timelines in sand. You may find that, like the tortoise in the famous Aesop fable, the slower approach is actually faster in the long run.

Summary

You've discovered the core change tools in this chapter. Whether you've dipped in and found the one you need for now, or read through them all, they are here for you to return to. I also imagine that you've realised that some of them could be helpful to friends and family as they also face change, so feel free to share with them if any tools feel particularly helpful. Here's a quick reminder of the tools in this chapter. You might even choose to work on one a week for the next two months to grow what you have access to:

- Making the vision tangible – creating a vision board
- The power of questions and enquiry
- Getting to know your gremlins or inner allies
- Asking for help
- Accountability to bust your own BS
- Gratitude – the antidote to guilt
- Mindfulness
- Feelings and needs
- Slowing down to speed up

Notes

Lost

David Wagoner, *Traveling Light: Collected and New Poems*

Stand still. The trees ahead and bushes beside you
Are not lost. Wherever you are is called Here,
And you must treat it as a powerful stranger,
Must ask permission to know it and be known.
The forest breathes. Listen. It answers,
I have made this place around you,
If you leave it you may come back again, saying Here.
No two trees are the same to Raven.
No two branches are the same to Wren.
If what a tree or a bush does is lost on you,
You are surely lost. Stand still.
The forest knows where you are
You must let it find you.

Your Key Insights

Use this page to capture your key takeaways from reading and working through *Untangled* for this particular change. You can share this with me at www.untangledbook.com/myinsight . I'd love to hear what's new for you and where you might still have questions to explore.

My key insight

What I understand now

What difference it's made

What I'm still wondering

Some Final Words

So here we are. The final pages of this book. An ending, of sorts. But in reality, it's just the beginning. As you've read through the chapters, you've deepened your understanding of yourself. Starting with a tangled mess, you've teased apart the threads and discovered more of what's here for you now.

What you know now is different to what you knew at the start. You've faced change that you've chosen and the stuff that you haven't. Each chapter of your life from here on will be different because of the work you've done here. You can become more intentional and conscious of the choices you make. You've strengthened your courage and your resilience. Through each journalling prompt, or each experiment with change in your own life, you've given yourself more to draw on. Although it

I'm proud of you. Of who you are and of who you are becoming

might sound strange, I'm proud of you. Because I know that to look in the metaphorical mirror and see who you are now and what you want, is not easy. And you've done it. You're doing it. You've taken the steps. You've faced your fears. You have lived through change. So yes, I might never have met you.

And yes, I'm proud of you. Of who you are and of who you are becoming. You are giving yourself the tools and skills to choose to untangle the threads of your life and weave with intention. You are picking up those threads and choosing how to live with meaning and purpose. You are choosing meaningful change. One thread at a time. One thought at a time. You are changing your life.

Take a minute now to share with me one piece of insight you've gained from this book – the thread that's most untangled for you right now. Upload it at *www.untangledbook.com/myinsight* and I'll share it back with you as a reminder in the future. You'll also have the chance to opt in to receive more insight and thoughts from me through my weekly change chats.

I would love to hear how you've progressed. It makes me smile to get emails that tell me of the changes you've faced and who you've become in the process. It's my deepest wish that you are able to live the life of your dreams and I am grateful that you've allowed me to be part of that. My own story will no doubt continue to become tangled and untangled, over and over. The threads that are here now will evolve and change, and I will continue to share those for the sake of reminding you that you are not alone and to help you with your own tangles.

Keep untangling.

Kirsty

ADDITIONAL NOTES

The Poems I Chose and Why I Chose Them

Atticus Poetry: A Tangled Mess

It's me, a beautiful, tangled mess. It's also everyone I've ever known or worked with. I'm fascinated by the tangled mess in each of us, and my life's mission is to help you untangle those knots, with love, care and compassion. I'll sit, cross-legged, for as long as it takes.

Morgan Harper Nichols: Perspective

I love the work of Morgan Harper Nichols. She writes from the heart and speaks directly to some of what I need. In the context of what we choose as we live through change, it feels important to remind you that nothing is forever. People change; seasons change. Your perspective changes too. If things feel tough, they won't always feel like this.

David Whyte: Start Close In

I often read this poem to clients when they're facing big and daunting change. There's always the step we don't want to take and, unfortunately, that step is often the one we need to start with. David Whyte works as an organisational poet and has a beautiful voice to listen to. I recommend listening to him reading his own work to bring a new depth and meaning to the words.

Eleanor Farjeon: There Are Big Waves

My dad used to read poems to us when we were children. This was always one of my favourites and it remains so now. You can ride the waves, even the big ones that threaten to overwhelm you.

David Wagoner: Lost

I first heard this poem read at a workshop I attended many years ago. It acts as a powerful reminder that sometimes we just have to stand still and listen. We are never truly lost.

Untangled in Organisations

This book has emphasised change for individuals, the myths you believe, the clarity that helps, how to connect with your own self and choose what works for you in the context of your wider life. As I've shared, I've learned and tested these tools and approaches by working with thousands of people in organisations, at major companies like Sky, Johnson & Johnson, NHS Scotland, JP Morgan and Skyscanner.

Sometimes people ask me 'what about untangling problems in group dynamics?', and it's true. There are many, and it's the same process because organisations are groups of individuals. Everything at an individual level applies in groups and teams, plus the need to look at how those individuals connect, relate and operate with each other.

I remember being extremely nervous speaking at an event I did in June 2021. It was the biggest event I'd ever done a keynote presentation at, with an audience of five thousand people. I was terrified! My natural 'professional' self told me that I had to do a brilliant job, and that meant I had to be polished and professional, show no signs of nerves and just get on with the show. I vividly remember the feeling of nausea as I sat at my desk in the studio at the bottom of my garden, and the producer asked me if there was any reason we weren't ready to go live to an online audience of 5000 people. Honestly, in that moment I could think of tons of reasons, but I didn't think I could say any of them out loud! I took a deep breath in and, voice breaking slightly, said, 'No, it's fine.' The countdown started from ten, the last three numbers were silent, on the screen only, and I was live. And I told the audience, who I couldn't even see, that I was really scared. That this was tough.

Then I got on and delivered content that inspired, empowered and equipped each person to be braver in their leadership and to face change in their lives.

I still get emails years later telling me of the impact of that session, how much difference it made and how, in the space of an hour online, I created a shift for those individuals. And here's the thing. Yes, I was vulnerable – I told them I was scared. But I didn't share everything that was going on at that time. I shared what I was willing and able to share with them, in the context of that session and for a reason. I was vulnerable to a point. I told them I was nervous because it aligned with the key point of the workshop: that it's okay to not be perfect; it's important to give yourself permission. In essence, I busted the eighth change myth that change has to look good. I told them part of my story. I acknowledged how I felt and what I needed. I didn't tell them that I was still on bereavement leave, that my mum's funeral had been two weeks earlier. I didn't tell them I was barely sleeping at the time because they didn't need to know that. That didn't serve their learning needs. It's one of the biggest things we teach when we work with organisations to help them untangle change. Leaders who learn to be vulnerable without just sharing everything with no awareness of their impact, learn how to build stronger connections and increase trust in their teams and organisations. It's a skill – you can learn it, and it matters for untangling change in organisations.

As a manager or leader, you also want a culture that's collaborative, where people take ownership of things and work together to achieve the overall outcomes of the organisation. You want them to be responsible, to raise issues directly with each other, rather than constantly come to you for the solutions, and you want them to ask for help when they need it. So, in unravelling the knots of change in organisations, the first step is to get to know yourselves and each other more. To take the content of the connect step from Chapter 2 and work with it in your team.

It reminds me of a time many years ago when I worked with a manager called Steve. Steve worked in financial services, and his team were great people – they were all good at their jobs and had been successful in their careers. They were also all exceptional at doing things by themselves. But when it came to collaboration and effectively working together, they struggled. Any time they had issues with each other, they took them to Steve rather than talking to each other. Steve often felt like he was running a playground rather than a senior leadership team. He asked me to run a workshop for his team, and we started with one basic principle: get to know each other. In the workshop we used two core tools: 'what's the story so far?', which helped them to see each other and their backgrounds and context as a starting point, and 'how do you feel and what do you need?' as a practice they could embed in their regular team meetings. We taught them how to start each meeting by checking in with how they were feeling and what they needed so that they connected as human beings first and then moved on to the work. It's a five-minute

Within a few weeks, they started to trust each other more; they were more easily able to challenge each other activity, and it brought them a complete transformation. Within a few weeks, they started to trust each other more; they were more easily able to challenge each other when things weren't right; and Steve was finally able to become more strategic, knowing that he could rely on his team to deliver, to raise issues with each other and to come to him only when he actually needed to be involved. The organisation around Steve's team noticed the difference and started to ask him what the secret sauce was! The power of untangling in a team extends way beyond the team itself into the wider organisation, if you let it.

Untangled 5% Club

Five per cent of all proceeds from the sale of Untangled products are donated to charity partners who support people from vulnerable, marginalised and minority groups as they face change in their lives.

To find out more, or to nominate a charity, visit www.untangledbook.com/charity

Untangled Acknowledgements

'Feeling gratitude and not expressing it is like wrapping a present and not giving it.' (William Arthur Ward).

These feel like the hardest pages of the book to write because if you've been in my life in any way, shape or form, you've influenced me and you've therefore influenced this book, for which I am grateful. So I'd like you to imagine a huge stage, with all of you on it, taking a bow, while I cheer you on from the audience and express my thanks for the contribution you've made. If our paths have crossed you are in that ensemble, receiving my gratitude and acknowledgments for playing your part in this human existence.

And there are some of you who have played lead roles, whom I'd like to specifically acknowledge because of the way you've shaped me and my life.

Firstly to those who've shaped me:

My Family: You've heard some things about my mum throughout this book and tragically she's not here to see the final product. Mum and I were more similar than I realised until shortly before she died, so her fingerprints are definitely throughout this book and she's left part of her legacy through me. My dad has also undoubtedly shaped who I am, and continues to do so as we live on without mum. I'm fortunate to have had two strong parents who started me off with a love of books, and the rest is history.

Whilst they haven't been specifically mentioned in Untangled, there are two formidable women I've had the pleasure to know for all of their lives. My middle sister Jenny and my little sister Hazel have become my absolute rocks in life, and I am beyond grateful that we have each other. I might have tortured them when we were kids, but we've grown beyond that and our threads weave magic in the world, whether over cocktails and giggles or a mutual support with creative endeavours. I love you both dearly.

And Scarlet, you've shown me what love is and through you I've become a better person. Having you in my life is a gift and I'm grateful that we get to live through tangles together. Love you Sweet Pea.

My Friends: Friends are the family we choose, the people we travel with and who we connect with for a reason, a season, or a lifetime. All of my friends have to put up with my continual pursuit for growth, learning and self-development. I want to pay specific thanks to Carolyn, Kate, Amber, Jane, Jenn, Sarah, Lara, Erica, AJC, Edith, Sheryne, Coeni and Scott, each of whom have supported me in different ways. Whether it be recently or a long time ago, for a long time or a short time, you've made your mark on my life and I'm thankful for that, even if we are not currently deeply connected.

Now to those who've guided and supported my work in the world:

- I have intentionally sought out coaches and mentors throughout my life, people who could help me to step fully into my potential. Each one has brought me something different, and I express my thanks here to Rama, Andrew, Helen, Jo, Ian, Laurie, Molly, Brynne and Patty, as well as to my counsellors and therapists over the years.

- A business like Firefly, which I created in order to make a difference in the world, doesn't take flight without the trust of clients and those who come into the business to play their part. To our clients and Firefly Team, past, present and future, thank you for seeing my vision, for trusting me to lead you into that and for playing your part in continually evolving the work I do in the world. You help me to live out my purpose in life and I'm grateful that I can do so in such stellar company.

Running a business can be lonely and I rely on professional communities to bounce ideas, huddle together for mutual support and to continually challenge my thinking. Specific thanks to my Co-Active leadership tribe, the Certified Dare to Lead(™) Facilitators community, the global Co-Active coach network and my former consulting networks.

I am also beyond grateful for the Transformational Leadership Council members who've come into my life at the right time, and helped me to recognise more fully the gifts and talent I bring to the world. It's an honour to become part of this collective and to offer my service and support to each of you.

I also want to acknowledge with gratitude the angels, souls and spirits who guide me in the world and in this work. Sometimes the smallest glimmer has created a tiny adaptation in my work, sometimes it's been a seismic shift. I'm always connected to something bigger and am held with love and intention.

And thirdly to those who've encouraged me with this book and moulded it into its present form:

In 2020 I ran two workshops with the Scottish Women's Development Forum in Police Scotland. Though I'd planned to write a book for several years, that day in lockdown was the catalyst for Untangled. To each of those participants who shared with vulnerability and told me what you dreamed of, this book is for you. It's the resource I wanted to be able to point you to at the end of our time together - thanks for waiting patiently for three years while it came to life!

Books can be written, and books are there to be shared. The first group of people I shared the full manuscript with helped me to improve and re-shape this book, to the Brilliant Beta Readers, you may not know how terrifying it was to send that email to you with the manuscript, but I'm grateful for your comments, feedback, notes and suggestions. You'll recognise some of those in this final version.

If you follow me on Instagram or LinkedIn then every time you click 'like' or comment on something, you're shaping my work in the world. I'm committed to bringing you content that inspires, is relatable and practical and makes a difference in your lives. Thank you for trusting me to do that.

This book would not be the book that it is without the invaluable support of those who know how to get books into the world: Steve Harrison and his team, Beth Kempton and the team at Troubador. Beth's book proposal masterclass helped me to turn my 'blob' of an idea into a full plan. Steve's team has helped me to up level this book and make it the best I can be, specific thanks to Deb, Geoffrey, Sarah and Steve. It's been a long journey, and it's been worth it. The team at Troubador has given me the path to get words into reality. Stuart at Jericho Writers deserves a special mention for making me laugh through editing which is no mean feat! Melanie Gee at Words and Indexes brought tears to my eyes with the index (in a good way) which totally surprised me. And Stacey MacDonald fiercely held my feet to the metaphorical fire in helping me bring my personal stories to life in these pages. There were tears and there was swearing, and I'm grateful.

Suz, Bhavini, Abi and Lacey, you have been the unstoppable force that has really got this thing out into the world! You each know the difference you've made and I'm applauding you from here. Keep on bringing your brilliance.

And finally, my thanks to you, who've trusted me to be your guide as you step more fully into living purposefully though change. Life is full of change, find those who you will cheer on for the part they play in your existence, and receive the applause with a smile when others thank you for being part of theirs.

My heartfelt thanks,

Kirsty

About the Cover Artwork

I was delighted to commission Kindah Khalidy for the cover artwork for *Untangled*. The beauty of her work is in the messy imperfections, and it felt completely right for this book. Here are Kindah's own words about the piece:

My focus for the cover artwork for Untangled *was to create balance and accentuate the beauty in the layers and 'tangles'.*

Kindah Khalidy

www.kindahkhalidy.com

Author Headshot: Donna Green Photography

Resources

The following resources have been referenced in Untangled and the poems shared with permission. Each of these books are highly recommended if you want to explore further and read more about some of the tools and skills I've highlighted in Untangled or immerse yourself in some of the great poetry that's influenced me.

Atticus 'Tangled Mess' in Love Her Wild, Headline (2017)

Bain, Barnet The Book of Being and Doing: Rediscovering Creativity in Life, Love and Work Atria (2015)

Brown, Brené Daring Greatly: How the Courage to Be Vulnerable Transforms the Way We Live, Love, Parent and Lead Penguin Life (2015)

Brown, Brené Rising Strong, Vermillion (2015)

Brown, Brené Dare to Lead: Brave Work. Tough Conversations. Whole Hearts Random House (2018)

Canfield, Jack with Switzer, Janet The Success Principles, Harper (2005)

Clear, James Atomic Habits: An Easy & Proven Way to Build Good Habits & Break Bad Ones, Random House (2018)

Covey, Stephen M. R. Trust and Inspire, Simon & Schuster (2022)

Covey, Stephen R. First Things First, Simon & Schuster (1999)

Farjeon, Eleanor 'There are Big Waves', in The Children's Bells, Oxford University Press (1957)

Gilbert, Elizabeth Big Magic: How to Live a Creative Life, and Let Go of Your Fear, Bloomsbury (2016)

Neff, Kristin *Fierce Self-Compassion: How Women Can Harness Kindness to Speak Up, Claim Their Power and Thrive*, Penguin Life (2021)

Nichols, Morgan Harper *'Perspective' in All Along You Were Blooming: Thoughts For Boundless Living*, Zondervan (2020)

Nichols, Lisa & Switzer, Janet *Abundance Now: Amplify Your Life & Achieve Prosperity Today*, Dey Street Books (2017)

Oliver, Mary *'The Summer Day'* in House of Light, Beacon Press (1992)

Rosen, Michael *We're Going on a Bear Hunt*, Walker Books (2015)

Rosenberg, Marshall *Non-Violent Communication - A Language of Life: Life-Changing Tools for Healthy Relationships*, Puddle Dancer Press (2015)

Sinek, Simon *Start With Why: How Great Leaders Inspire Everyone To Take Action*, Penguin (2011)

Sprake, Colin *Entrepreneur Success Recipe*, Morgan James Publishing (2013)

Misner, Ivan; Phillips, Dawa & Giusto, Heidi *The Third Paradigm: A Radical Shift to Greater Success*, Entrepreneur Press (2023)

Wagoner, David *'Lost' in Traveling Light: Collected and New Poems*, University of Illinois Press (1999)

David Whyte, *'Start Close In' in River Flow: New and Selected Poems* Many Rivers Press (2012)

Index

About the Author

Navigating change has been part of Kirsty Maynor's professional and personal life for more than three decades. As a sought after change strategist, leadership consultant, single mum and someone who has faced divorce, debt, depression and disaster, survivor Kirsty Maynor has traversed some of life's most difficult transitions and emerged happier, smarter and more fulfilled with her resulting career and lifestyle changes.

Kirsty Maynor knows what it takes to face a crisis and create better-than-expected outcomes. Now, her simple approach to excelling in the face of change underpins her development work with multinational corporations, executive coaching clients and audiences around the world.

An accomplished coach – certified by the International Coaching Federation with an MSc in organisational behaviour, among numerous other professional credentials – Kirsty is also an award-winning entrepreneur who has dedicated her professional career to helping others live the life of their dreams. The coach to the coaches, she combines years of real-world experiences with advanced study in the field of human potential to coach elite corporate leaders, helping them determine what matters most, then creating future careers (and lifestyles) based on those decisions.

Kirsty is the first Scottish member of the exclusive global Transformational Leadership Council.

Additionally, Kirsty was the first certified facilitator in Scotland of Dr Brené Brown's Dare to Lead™ methodology.

Connect with Kirsty

Instagram: kirstymaynor
Facebook: Kirsty Maynor – Author
LinkedIn: Kirsty Maynor
www.kirstymaynor.com

How To Use Untangled in Organisations

Facing tangles of change in your organisation? Dealing with externally driven change or internally created evolution? Encountering resistance and barriers to change or just feeling a little lost?

Download your guide to Untangled for Organisations at www.untangledbook.com/organisations

Kirsty and her elite team at The Firefly Group (*www.thefireflygroup.co.uk*) have been the partner of choice for countless client organisations including Sky, NHS Scotland, Janssen, Haleon, JP Morgan, Scottish Government, MOD, Simon Community and Skyscanner. Over the last twenty-five years, Kirsty has:

- Advised national governments on key strategic decisions
- Led large corporations through significant strategic change programmes
- Supported the creation of coaching cultures in organisations
- Transformed collaboration and partnerships across industries

Kirsty's combined personal and professional experience is her superpower. The resulting synergy creates a unique perspective and an innovative but proven approach to change. It starts with the individual human in the context of the wider organisation and moves to the ultimate ripple effect into society.

The key principles of *Untangled* sit at the heart of each of these culture transformations. To bring this to your team or organisation through Firefly's work, contact the team at hello@thefireflygroup.co.uk for an introductory conversation.

Firefly partners with organisations facing change and delivers tangible improvements to your key organisation outcomes.

Firefly coaches, facilitators and change strategists deliver:

- Inspirational and action-oriented keynote speaking sessions
- Senior leadership coaching and development programmes
- Group coaching
- Internal mentor coaching and coaching supervision
- Online learning programmes designed for frontline staff and team leaders

If you're serious about change, it's time to talk.

Notes

Notes